SCAR ACROSS THE HEART

Bob Prouty

Pacific Press Publishing Association
Boise, Idaho
Montemorelos, Nuevo Leon, Mexico
Oshawa, Ontario, Canada

Edited by Don Mansell
Designed by Tim Larson
Cover by Sue Rother
Type set in Century Schoolbook

First printing 1986

Library of Congress Cataloging in Publication Data

Prouty, Robert.
Scar across the heart.

1. Prouty, Robert. 2. Missionaries—Zaire—
Biography. 3. Missionaries—United States—Biography.
4. Seventh-day Adventistis—Missions—Zaire. I. Title.
BV3625.C63P724 1986 266'.6732'0924 [B] 85-32086

ISBN 0-8163-0629-X

Dedication

noble (no′ bəl) adj.   Worthy, of exalted character.

foster (fos′ tər) tr.v.   To promote development or growth.

To the late Jason Noble, who was; to Roland and Agnes Foster, who did; and to the people of Lukanga.

Contents

Chapter 1

A Matter of Money

There are people in this world for whom $25,000 one way or the other would probably not even be noticed, or for whom, at best, it would mean very little. But I'm not one of them. And, judging from the voice on the other end of the line, my bank manager wasn't either. That's why he was calling me long distance. He wanted his money back.

I suspect it was the timing of the thing that had him worried the most. Diane and I were getting ready to head back to Africa, to our home at Lukanga in the Kivu province of Zaire. Our furlough was not quite over, but we had decided to go back early—two weeks early. When he called us, we had only one day left. So he was understandably nervous.

We had moved up the date of our return because of the school year in Zaire. Of course, our bank manager didn't know that. He didn't know that for missionaries on furlough the school year is always a problem, that the summer break is for two months while furlough is for three. All he knew was that we were leaving in a rush and we had his money—a lot of it.

The last month of a furlough is a lot like the first three weeks of December. You spend your days shopping, your evenings wrapping, and your nights planning—but Christmas doesn't come. Oh, I suppose it does, in a way, for there's great excitement at being so close to getting back, but there's great regret as well. A thousand days of separation from family and friends loom very large from this perspective, especially when your only contact is by mail and the mail takes at least a month to get through.

We didn't know, as the last few hours slipped away, that there was a banker for whom the thought of separation was almost as painful as it was for us. We didn't know that he was desperately phoning different members of our family, trying to locate us before we left. And we certainly didn't know why he wanted to talk to us, but we were soon to find out. It wasn't to say Bon voyage, I can assure you.

Earlier in the day, one of his tellers had made an error in our favor! On my way out of Oshawa for the last time, I had stopped at the bank to withdraw $2,500 for a money order to pay for shipping our baggage, our motorcycle, and several other items. The teller made out the money order as I requested, but then she made a *slight* error, a little nothing, really. Instead of $2,500, she typed in $25,000. I didn't notice it.

I left for Michigan when I finished my transaction at the bank, and it was late that night before the manager's phone call reached me. He was doing his best to sound casual.

"There's been a small error with that money order you got from us," he said, the worry in his voice almost palpable. "Did you cash it yet?"

"No," I answered, "I wasn't planning to cash it until tomorrow."

"Oh, good," he said, answering just a little too hastily to sound natural. "The teller made a mistake, and you might have had trouble getting it cashed. We wouldn't want that, would we?"

"No," I agreed, "we certainly wouldn't."

He went on expansively. "Tell you what. Just to make sure you have no problems, I'll send my assistant down there with a new money order tonight."

"But it's a 300-mile drive down here," I protested. "It would take him the whole night."

"I know, I know," he acknowledged. "But it's the least we can do. After all, the error was ours, not yours. And we certainly don't want to have you running into problems at the last minute." A bank manager was there to serve the bank's customers, and if it meant driving all night, well, that was just the way it would have to be.

Call me a realist if you will, or a cynic if you must, but to my suspicious ears, something didn't sound quite right. I made a motion to Diane, who was standing nearby trying to figure out the whole conversation from the half she could hear. "Bring me the money order," I whispered.

The banker was still talking when she came back, and I looked at the money order with great curiosity. It wasn't until three or four apologies later that I finally noticed the mistake. It was surprising how inconspicuous it was, really—until you had seen it, that is. After that, it was hard to take your eyes off it again. I pointed it out to my wife as the man talked on, assuring me for the fifth or maybe the sixth time of his bank's earnest desire to be of service.

Diane says I let him off the hook too easily. I don't know. Maybe I did. But I let it pass. I didn't bother to point out to him that I could have cashed the thing anywhere in the world and there would have been no questions asked. But he should have known a missionary wouldn't do such a thing. In the end I simply had him send the corrected amount to a nearby bank just over the border in Canada, and he paid me mileage to drop off the old money order and pick up the new one.

We left for Zaire the next day. The bill for the shipment came to $2,462, and I counted the change carefully before putting it into my wallet. It would come in handy during the trip, and after what had just happened, I didn't want any more mistakes. You see, there are people in this world for whom $38 one way or the other would probably not even be noticed, or for whom, at best, it would mean very little. But I'm not one of them.

Chapter 2

Kicking Up a Storm

There was a certain satisfaction coming back to Lukanga as a second-term missionary, a certain sense of reassurance. I felt that at last I was starting to make some small degree of progress. I had three years of experience to draw on now. I had trudged hundreds of miles through the nearby hills and preached dozens of sermons. I had taught thousands of classes in French and had finally learned to speak Swahili. More important, I was getting to know people, and people were getting to know me. They greeted me by name in the villages now as I passed through, and I was able to stop and converse, where before I had been limited to greetings. Yet the more I grew to know the people, the more deeply I felt the gulf that separated us; and the more I learned, the stronger was my impression that I knew almost nothing at all.

We had scarcely settled in for the new school year when a fresh problem came to the fore at the primary school, which made me feel my inabilities even more than I had in the past. The problem was the harshness of discipline in some of the classrooms. Several of the new teachers were using their rulers for more than measuring. They were pandying the students with them. Incorrect answers and homework undone would be handled by a sharp rap on the outstretched palm with a ruler.

It was a delicate situation. I had been directly in charge of the primary school the year before, but now the job was Nzalita's. That had been my idea. Ever since I'd come here, I'd been pushing for placing the most competent national workers in positions of responsibility. If I were to intervene now, I might be able to solve the immediate problem, but what would happen over the long run? For Nzalita to reach his full potential as an administrator, he needed the freedom to make his own decisions, and learn from his successes and failures as he went along. He needed to be trusted. And yet, my students at the secondary school were preparing to be teachers themselves. They did most of their observing and practice teaching at the primary school and I was concerned that they would pick up bad habits by watching the hand whackings. Thinking it over, I decided a few words of advice might be in order.

"Nzalita," I said. "I hear some of the teachers are whacking the hands of the students who give the wrong answers."

Yes, he allowed, he had also heard of it.

"What do you think of it?" I asked, prodding just a little.

He didn't like the idea, he said, but it was hard to know what to do. Teachers in other schools did it all the time.

"But we can't condone violence in the classrooms," I said. "We've always taught in this school that there are far better ways of handling situations."

Yes, he agreed, that was so, but if he tried to come down too hard on the teachers, they would say he wasn't really in charge but was just doing whatever I told him to do. And then there'd be no end of problems.

I wasn't ready to give up yet. "Maybe you could just talk with them and tell them what *you* think," I continued.

"Oh, I have," he said. "They tell me that it's easy for me to say what I tell them because I don't have to spend the whole day in the classroom as they do."

"All right," I said, relenting, "but see what you can do. I really don't want it to continue."

He walked out of my office doubtless feeling even more frustrated than I did. A principal's job is complicated at the best of times and next to impossible at others. Unless your teachers feel that you're supporting them, you're going nowhere. And unless you see that students are dealt with fairly and professionally, you'll be going in the wrong direction.

My frustration grew as the weeks went by and the problem

persisted. Nzalita had counseled his teachers, and while they always listened politely, they weren't convinced. "This is only going to lead to more problems," he had told them, but the tide of opinion was against him, and he felt he couldn't push his point any further.

I held a general meeting with the primary-school staff every month that year, and I never failed to offer my opinion regarding the hand whacking. But it was a nonissue with most of the teachers, and, as the months went by, I felt I was getting nowhere. But unbeknown to me, help was on the way—help in the form of an irate parent.

Her name was Mutunzi (the name means "storm"). It couldn't have been more appropriate, for she was a little whirlwind of thunder and lightning. Her son had come home the day before with sore knuckles from being rapped with the ruler. It was punishment for an incomplete homework assignment. I had somehow assumed that the parents knew about the hand whacking and were in basic agreement with the idea, but obviously, I was wrong. The students had been keeping their problems to themselves, probably fearing a repeat performance at home if they didn't. So when Mutunzi heard what had happened to her son and learned that it wasn't the first time he had been punished, it came as a complete surprise, and she decided to take matters into her own hands.

She kept her son home from school the next day and, sometime between recess and the noon-hour break, she showed up herself. Arriving in the courtyard at the front of the school, she realized she didn't know which classroom was her son's, so spotting a young first-grader wandering by on his way to the outdoor toilet, she collared him for the information. He, of course, realized at once that this would be no ordinary visit and pointed out the door with delight. Then he followed along behind, eyes wide with anticipation but careful to keep out of range of any stray blows which might chance to fall.

It was just as well. As soon as he indicated the classroom, the tirade began. The teacher was not even within earshot and already Mutunzi was working herself into top form. Several of the village women, passing by on their way to the fields, heard the commotion and came over for a closer look. They weren't sure just what the particular problem was, but one issue was as good as another, and their indignant mutterings added to the growing babble of voices outside the little school. The little first-grader by now had completely forgotten why he was outside in the first place and waited hopefully, with his nose pressed flat against the classroom window to see what would happen. He wasn't disappointed.

The teacher saw the commotion and heard the little group approaching his door. He was genuinely frightened, for it sounded like a sizable mob. But when the door flew open and he saw that it was only Mutunzi and a few of her friends, he was still staggered by the force of the verbal onslaught. She walked right up to him, eyes flashing with the indignation that only a mother could so eloquently feel, and thrust her face forward close to his. He flinched instinctively under her assault and stepped backward, stumbling over a desk in his haste. Mutunzi continued to advance aggressively until their faces almost touched and the hapless teacher retreated as far as he could. Pressed flat against the blackboard, he had no place else to go except sideways. As he tried to slip away he left two wide swaths where he wiped the board clean with his shoulders and the seat of his pants. But his efforts were in vain, for Mutunzi had backed him into a corner. Escape was impossible, and the pelting hail of her words continued unabated. Big faces and little pressed up against all of the windows now, peering in, with new on-lookers multiplying as if by magic. And why not? This would be a story to tell and retell around the family fires for weeks to come.

Her quarry firmly trapped in the corner, Mutunzi momentarily paused, no longer sure what to do with her victim. As she paused to catch her breath and look around, the teacher straightened up and tried to regain his composure as he brushed off his clothes, hopeful that the storm had passed. But Mutunzi's hesitation was only momentary. Catching her second wind and doubtless fortified by the encouraging smiles of the onlookers, she staggered the teacher with a fresh verbal barrage. Then lashing out with her bare feet, she struck the teacher squarely in the shins. He jumped up and yelped in pain. Gratified by his reaction, Mutunzi tried a repeat performance and achieved the same results. This was victory, complete and uncontested, and she could ask for no more. Turning triumphantly on her heel, she strode out of the classroom, her head held high.

Only now did the teacher look up. Noticing the faces at the window for the first time, he gestured at them menacingly and they all disappeared just as suddenly as they had appeared.

The excitement over, the students resumed their seats and the teacher returned to his teaching. He made a few ill-tempered remarks about the "crazy village women," then carried on, pretending to be unaffected by what had happened. And maybe he was unaffected. Maybe only the students were affected. Maybe from that day forward they all did their homework on time and gave the right answers in class. I don't know, but for whatever reason, from that day forward there was no more violence in the classrooms. Hand whacking had ended for good.

Chapter 3

In Committee

The long grass in the boundless flat fields around Lubumbashi lay faded and brown, and the termite hills, like silent sentinels, stood watch over a lifeless landscape. Not a blade of grass moved in all that vast panorama, not a breath of air disturbed the oppressive stillness. It was late November. No rain had fallen for months, and all of nature was waiting for the first few drops to herald the end of the dry season and awaken the slumbering countryside. Red clouds of choking dust chased our car whenever we strayed from the main roads, and the parched fields were cracked like an ancient painting. In the pallid sky above, tired clouds stretched long and listless from one distant horizon to the other, and the passing days brought no hope of rain.

It was committee time in Lubumbashi, and at church headquarters, the weather was taking its toll. All around the long mahogany tables in the board room, heads were beginning to nod. Flies droned dispiritedly against the windowpanes, and the room was heavy with ennui. Never had I been to a series of meetings so completely pervaded by the spirit of the season. The dryness in the air seemed to permeate everything, and as report followed wearying report, I found my thoughts beginning to wander, slipping back over the long miles and the desolate landscape to the lush green hills of Kivu.

There's an attractiveness, an appealing freshness, about the Kivu that never seems to fade with the passage of time. The streams never lose their sparkle nor the little groves their charm. There are new delights to be discovered around each bend in the path, and there are old haunts to be enjoyed time and again. The Kivu is home. It's where I belong, and I find myself more and more reluctant to leave, be it only for the shortest of time or for the best of reasons. Year-end committees seem to be neither.

There are those who enjoy committees, who revel in the reports and find positive pleasure in the endless passing of policy papers. They come into the board room with an air of anticipation and arrange their papers with solemn dignity. I watch their comings and goings with a twinge of envy, for I wasn't made that way. Committees for me are ordeals, something to be borne with as much good grace as possible, and I find myself begrudging every minute I spend in them.

It's not that they don't have their exciting moments. Sometimes they do. Sometimes there is a quick burst of opinions, springing up from nowhere like a flock of birds suddenly taking wing. Then the board room becomes a moving, living place, filled with noise and chatter as suggestions and ideas fly back and forth. Such moments don't last for long and they don't occur often, but just knowing they are possible keeps me going when the pace slackens and I find my attention beginning to wane.

We follow the same format each year. Our meetings start promptly at eight in the morning. A siren sounds about five minutes before the hour—reveille for some by the way they rushed in late—and we start making our way to the board room. For those of us who lodge in the guest rooms on the second floor, this means we have to go past a magazine rack standing at the top of the stairs. That rack is positioned in a very strategic spot. It's a temptation, and one to which many a delegate has succumbed.

As we took our places around the long tables one morning, I couldn't help but notice that Leif Hansen, our union publishing secretary, had been the latest to yield. He had a *Reader's Digest* tucked under his agenda sheet.

Leif was responsible for book sales and promotion, and his interest in reading material was therefore thoroughly understandable, even commendable. The issue of the magazine he had chosen had some especially interesting articles as I could personally attest from the previous day's committee.

Leif and I thought alike on many issues. We had hit it off well from the time we first met. That was when he came to Lukanga to hold a Week of Prayer for the students. I remember being impressed with his straightforwardness and sincerity.

As I watched him now across the table, reading surreptitiously, I saw a chance for a bit of good-natured ribbing. I felt I simply couldn't pass up the opportunity. I have always fancied myself to be something of a minor poet, and the muse struck me suddenly and irresistibly that morning. For various obscure reasons, it had become accepted practice for committee members to stand during certain important votes, so I dashed off a few verses dedicated to Leif about the problems to which this could lead.

'Twas the month before Christmas at year-end committee.
The chairman was speaking, but oh what a pity!
As Leif sat there reading his *Digest* with care
The good chairman asked him to open with prayer.
Poor Leif hadn't heard—as we rose to our feet
His ears looked like crimson, his face like a beet.
He thought, "Well, it must be we're standing to vote
And they want my opinion," so he first cleared his throat.
Then he said, "I'm not sure just what you've proposed,
But I want you to know that I'm firmly opposed."

I folded the poem carefully, scribbled Leif's name, and passed the note to the person on my left. He passed it to the delegate beside him and so it went, from hand to hand around the board table, each person in turn treating it with the deepest respect, as if it were an important communiqué. Many such notes are passed solemnly back and forth during the course of the proceedings, and I often wonder what they contain. Most of them are doubtless important, but I suspect that some of them are of no more consequence than mine.

Leif got my message and, apparently repentant, put down his *Digest* and took up his pen. A few minutes later, another note was working its way from hand to hand around the table, this time in the opposite direction. Leif had wasted no time in evening the score, and I soon found myself reading a pointed poem about my fondness for casual clothes.

'Twas the eve of committees and time for the ball—
That wonderful feast that is cherished by all.
The tables by candlelight glittered so bright,
With crystal and china reflecting the sight.
The spoons were of silver, the knives were of gold.
The whole place was reeking with riches untold.
The men in tuxedos, the ladies in gowns
Had just strutted in and had sat themselves down
When the doorway was darkened, a man sauntered in
With T-shirt and tennies, and lop-sided grin.
The ladies were sobbing, the men did perspire,
For 'twas Bob in his usual meeting attire!

It was not long after this exchange of doggerel that I noticed the pace of the meeting began to liven up. Committee members seem to have a sixth sense to tell them when something important is about to happen and, as if by some silent signal, poems and letters were quickly put away, the whispered conversations came to an abrupt halt.

Suddenly, every word the chairman said was meaningful, every nuance of expression analyzed. A motion was made, and the discussion started to flow. There was an exhilarating rush of opinions, and we strained forward in our chairs to catch it all. The arguments were forceful and every moment instructive. Then suddenly, unexpectedly, the chairman rose to his feet.

The job of a chairman is a difficult one, maybe even, at times, an impossible one. Everyone wants a chance to talk. Everyone deserves a chance to talk. Indeed, everyone should be encouraged to talk, yet it's the insistent ticktock from the wall behind him which often rings loudest in his ears. Schedules must be kept. The agenda must be covered, and somehow everything must be kept moving along. Each chairman has his own way of dealing with this problem, but our chairman's approach that morning was unique, I thought. He looked around the room, cleared his throat nervously a few times, conferred with the secretary, and finally spoke.

"According to the schedule on our agenda sheet, we've run out of time. We're due for a fifteen-minute recess right now. We feel that the motion before us is an important one, and we want it out of the way before we break. We've had enough discussion, so let's go ahead with the vote. All those in favor of the motion, please stand while prayer is offered."

Well, no one ever said human beings were perfect. Things aren't always done as they should be done and mistakes occasionally are made. Harried chairmen must accept part of the blame. But I'm afraid that committee members who scribble satirical verse must bear their share of responsibility too.

Still the overall pattern is positive. Committees can have their frustrating moments, but they can be very rewarding as well. God's work continues to move ahead. Before our year-end committee meetings ended that year, the chairman had guided through some important actions and had inspired us with some thrilling calls to service. Oh, and one last observation . . . I don't know whether or not it is significant, but halfway through the session the long dry spell finally ended and the rain fell on the parched brown earth in abundance.

Chapter 4

Repeat Performance

A cold tide of panic began rising rapidly inside me as I looked around. Something was wrong. Kisanzi was supposed to be a little church with barely a hundred members, but I could see five times that number sprawled across the hillside before me—and that meant trouble.

I had been looking forward to this visit for weeks, ever since Kavis first invited me to preach. It was his uncle's home church. He described it as a dingy little building, with cobwebbed ceilings and cracked walls. I wasn't worried about that. I have always found it exciting to visit a place you haven't been before, and besides, the folks at Kisanzi hadn't heard my sermon on tithe-paying yet. That alone made the trip worthwhile.

You see, my grasp of the Nande language was tenuous at best. This meant that, when I preached, I had to follow my notes rather closely. I had only about five sermons worked up in Nande, and most of them were quite a struggle to deliver. But the sermon on tithe-paying was different. It was my pride and joy, my masterpiece. It contained all my favorite stories and texts, and long before the invitation to preach at Kisanzi, I had memorized every line of it, every text and every word. I had practiced it time and again, and I had it down pat. There was just one problem—everyone had heard it! I had preached it everywhere I had ever been—except Kisanzi. But now it looked as if there was a problem here too. Surely all of these people didn't belong to this one little church.

I scanned the crowd for faces I could recognize. There was

Kavis's uncle. He at least was from Kisanzi. And there was Kakule, smiling and raising his eyebrows in friendly greeting as I caught his eye. So far so good. But sitting beside him was Watolwa, and not far away was Mulyango. They were from Mageria, and old Number Four was just behind them. That was Murungi. He had been the fourth student to enroll at Lukanga when it started up years before, and it had taken him so long to finish that everyone just called him old Number Four. But he wasn't from Kisanzi either. He was from Mulema, and I didn't like the way things were beginning to look. Threading my way through the crowd, I quickly tracked down the church elder.

"Where did all these people come from?" I asked.

"Oh," he answered with a casual shrug of his shoulders, "around."

"Around where?" I continued.

"Around everywhere," he replied. "When we knew for sure you'd be coming, we decided to invite the other churches to join us."

"All of them?" I asked incredulously.

"Yes," he replied proudly, "all of them."

It was several moments before I found the courage to face my audience again. When I did, the first thing I noticed was the drab little church building in the background, half hidden by the trees. It looked even dingier than Kavis had described it to me, and somehow, now, that seemed to matter. The joy had gone out of the morning, and I sat glumly off to one side, waiting for my time to preach to arrive. This was going to be embarrassing, no doubt about it. If only I had put my five sermons together in one notebook as I had intended to do. Then I could at least choose a different topic.

As I pondered my predicament, my thoughts went to a church service held just a few months earlier. Pastor Kambale, one of our veteran workers, had faced a situation similar to mine and his response had been unique. This made me feel a little better, just thinking about it.

Pastor Kambale was an amazing person. There was no other way to describe him. All week long, he looked every bit his advanced age. When he went to his little garden down the hill from his home, his steps were slow and painful and he carried his hoe like a cane. When he wanted a drink of water from the spring, he no longer attempted to get it by himself but would ask one of the children to fill the little can he always carried. Even on Sabbaths, when he walked to church, it was with unsteady steps, and the pathway behind him would be congested with those who were too polite to pass him by.

It was the same in church. You couldn't help noticing that he was the last one to his knees for prayer and the last one to get up again. Whether it was because he no longer heard the amens or because his legs had grown weak or simply because he had a few private comments of his own to make to the Lord after prayer had been offered, no one ever knew, but he always stayed on his knees a good ten seconds after the Amen was pronounced. Only then would he work his way slowly into his pew.

But when it came time for him to preach, it was different. There was never any hesitating. He would spring to his feet, almost jumping at the pulpit. He would stride back and forth, gesturing and shouting, and his voice was strong. For forty-five minutes he was a young man again.

Preparing the sermons was a different story. This was hard for Pastor Kambale. There was no surge of energy, no burst of adrenalin. He found himself fighting all the infirmities of his age. And so, rather than work on new sermons, as he might have when he was young, he developed a collection of about ten, which had served him well over the years. These he bound together into a sort of book that he carried around wherever he went. He still visited some of the surrounding churches, a surprising number really, considering how difficult it had become for him to get around, and he always took his little book of sermons with him. It was as much a part of him as his Bible.

His system wasn't without its drawbacks. His memory wasn't what it had once been, and he had a hard time remembering where he had preached a given sermon. To avoid problems, he usually asked the local elder which sermon he had already preached in that particular church.

One day, as he strode up to the pulpit at the Rwese church, he suddenly realized that he had forgotten to confer with the local pastor. He had no idea which of his sermons they had heard, and which they had not. In a smaller church this would not have been much of a problem, but Rwese is a big church, with a thousand members, and it was packed. Nevertheless, completely undaunted, Pastor Kambale held his travelworn book of sermons high in one hand and announced the first title.

"Have you heard that one before?" he asked.

Yes, they shouted back, they'd heard it before.

He proceeded to the second sermon in the book and announced the title. "Have you heard this one before?"

Yes, they assured him, they'd heard that one too.

He called out the third title, the fourth, and the fifth, and, each time the answer was the same: "Yes, pastor, we've heard it." "Yes, pastor, yes." "You've preached it before."

When at last he'd exhausted his entire repertoire, there was a moment's pause as everyone waited to see what would happen next. Unabashed, he just held up the old book again.

"All right," he said, waving it in the air, "which one would you like to hear again?" A roar of laughter reverberated through the church, quickly followed by another as the votes were cast. Pastor Kambale waited calmly for quiet, announced the winning sermon, and proceeded to preach it.

I smiled to myself again as I thought about the incident. Pastor Kambale had a flair, all right. Not only had everyone listened to a sermon they had already heard, but they all went home feeling good about it. But it wasn't quite the same in my case. I knew I didn't have Pastor Kambale's flair for plowing ahead in spite of adverse circumstances, and I decided I'd better call the elder over again to ask his advice. He was unperturbed.

"What's the sermon about?" he asked.

"Paying tithe," I said.

He sounded pleased. "Good," he enthused, "go ahead and preach it. They need to hear it again, even if they've heard it before."

There are a lot of things I like about worship services in Africa, but I think it's the easy relationship between preacher and congregation that I like the best. It's something I've experienced time and again. When I've stumbled over a word, someone has always been ready to help me, and now, with a sermon that most of them had heard only weeks before, there wasn't a whisper of complaint. In fact, when I told them what I was going to do, there was a great roar of approval. Either they had enjoyed it so much the first time that they wanted to hear it again, or my foreign accent had baffled them entirely the first time around, and they wanted a second shot at it. To this day, I don't know which it was. I never had the courage to ask them, and they were kind enough never to say.

Chapter 5

Lucia and the Catholic Mission

Down the road and around the bend from our house, where the valley opens up and the hills recede in the distance, there's a cluster of red-brick buildings. This is the Catholic mission station run by Italian missionaries. The little boy who waves as you approach is an orphan named Mbusa. He lives at the mission station. He's the same age as my Danny, and the two are the best of friends. So are the two missions.

It's an unusual situation in many ways, for there are religious differences. There we are, almost side by side—Adventist mission, Catholic mission. By all the laws which are said to regulate such things, we ought to be in conflict all the time, but it hasn't worked out that way. Contrary to expectations, we work together, prayer together, and for almost ten years, groups from the two missions have been getting together on Monday nights to study the Bible together. We get together from time to time for spaghetti feeds too, and for games of Scusa.

Scusa is the Italian version of the parlor game Sorry. Only four at a time can play, but there is no limit to the number of those who can offer suggestions. This is always our favorite part of the game, and advice can usually be heard in any of five languages as the evening progresses—English, French, Italian, Swahili, and Nande. We joke that if two missions such as ours, with our religious differences, can play a game like Scusa "interdenominationalistically" and in five different languages, then there's hope for the warring nations of the world.

We have our own rules when we play Scusa. The most important is that play can never begin until there is a large bowl of tossed salad on the table—Italian dressing, of course. Giovanni is the salad specialist. He and Gianni run the Catholic mission. Both men are Italian priests with long years of experience in Africa. Gianni has a Ph.D. in psychology to go along with his theological studies, and, not surprisingly, he is the philosopher among the group. Giovanni is the practical one. Yet theory and practice combine when it comes to work, and both men seem as comfortable with the carpenter's apron as with their sacerdotal robes. Together they've put up an impressive number of buildings. They've worked on a great variety of projects, yet of everything they've done, nothing can be any more important than the maternity hospital.

Hospital? The word is perhaps too generous by most standards. At first glance, the building certainly doesn't look much like a hospital. It has just one story, with two wings, and somewhere in the process of construction, the masons miscalculated. The rows of bricks which make up the end wall of the east wing have a definite slant to them. It seems it was a question of mortar. The masons working on the left side of the door used a lot more of it than the masons working on the right side. But then, one can't worry too much about a little thing like that. Everything is solid and sturdy, and when there are visitors to be shown around Giovanni leans against the door in just a certain way, and no one really notices.

The building is crowded most of the time. The mamas, as everyone calls them, have been flocking to Lukanga to have their babies ever since it was built. Those who live at a distance are asked to come to Lukanga a month ahead of time. For most of them it's the only vacation they ever get. They bring along a sister or a niece or an older daughter to help prepare food and wash the clothes, and they get along very nicely. The nearest doctor is twenty kilometers (twelve and a half miles) away at Musienene, mind you, but the midwives are very competent and the care is constant. No matter that some of the patients must sleep in the hallway. No matter that medicines are scarce or that beds are hard. Love reigns in these halls, and by the standards of human love and caring, the word *hospital* is far too small, far too inadequate to describe what is going on here.

When the maternity hospital was built, there was a problem getting the bricks brought in. They had been purchased from a brickyard about fifteen kilometers (nine miles) away, but transportation was lacking. A number of our Adventist church members learned of the problem and spontaneously offered to help. Along with the local Catholic congregation, they carried tens of thousands of bricks over the hills on their heads. Goivanni was so impressed by their spirit of goodwill that he wrote up the story, and it was published in a Catholic weekly newspaper back in Italy.

With this history of sharing, it's not surprising that some of us at the Adventist mission are called on in times of emergency to rush a mama in labor to the hospital at Musienene. These are the bad cases, the sad cases, the cases where something has gone wrong. One night I was called on to rush a mama with a ruptured uterus over the roads to the doctor. She had already been carried by stretcher for seventeen hours before arriving at Lukanga, and it didn't look as if there were much hope for her, but she survived. She was one of the lucky ones. Lucia wasn't so fortunate.

Lucia didn't stay at the maternity hospital like so many of the mamas. She was from Lukanga, and so it was easy for her to come for regular checkups. The midwives all knew her, and she appeared to be doing fine. Besides, it wasn't her first pregnancy. It was her fifth or maybe her sixth. Concetta no longer remembers.

Concetta is in charge of the hospital. Originally from Sicily, she is an expert midwife herself and dedicated to the mamas. She knows them all by name and jokes with them as she walks through the building. She knows their children too and remembers when they were born, but there are some memories which are too painful for her to keep. One is the memory of Lucia.

When Lucia's day arrived, it looked at first that this delivery would have little to distinguish it from all of the others. The child was born without difficulty, and they named him Mbusa. He was healthy and well, but it soon became apparent that all was not well with Lucia. She needed help, more help than Concetta could give, and she needed it fast.

"*Povera [poor] donna,*" murmured Concetta. "It'll be all right." But in her heart she was far from sure. A vehicle was summoned, and within minutes they were in the old Land Rover, hurrying over the rough roads to Musienene, hoping against hope and praying that the doctor would be able to help.

One of the nurses at the Musienene hospital recognized the vehicle as it approached and hurried out to see what the problem was. Concetta explained quickly and started making preparations for Lucia to be carried in, but the nurse stopped her.

"It's no use," she said, shrugging her shoulders helplessly. "The doctor's not here. It's his day off, you know."

Yes, they knew, and there was nothing to do but to drive on another hour to Katwa. Only desperation could bring them to try the Katwa hospital. It had once had an excellent reputation, but by now, things were at an all-time low. It was poorly equipped by any standards. Medicine was nonexistent and nursing care almost nil. But Concetta had no alternative. Katwa at least had a doctor and an operating table.

Night had fallen by the time they arrived, and the hospital grounds were dark and quiet. This time, they had to hunt for the nurses, but when they found them, it was the same old story as before.

"Sorry, the doctor's not here. You know how it is." The same apologetic shrugging of the shoulders.

Yes, yes, they knew how it was. They also knew that Lucia was running out of time even faster than they were running out of hospitals, and as they drove off once again into the blackness of the night, searching for yet another hospital, they sensed that this time it would be too late.

In the back of the car, Concetta had been sitting by Lucia the whole time, talking softly in her beautiful mix of Italian and Swahili. She had cared for a lot of these women over the years, and still she marveled at their courage. Throughout the entire ordeal, with all the bouncing and jostling, Lucia had uttered not one word of complaint. It was a woman's lot to suffer, and she had known much suffering in her short life. Now she was tired and wanted only to rest. That rest, she knew, could not be long in coming.

Concetta knew it too, and her cheeks were warm with tears as she reached out to hold the brave little hand one last time. Lucia looked up and smiled faintly. Her eyes that had once shone like the bright glow of the full moon when the sky is clear and the drums beat loud were now dim like the last fading embers of a dying fire on a late and somber night.

"I'm going," she said calmly. "*Kwa heri* [Goodbye]." And with that, she closed her eyes and was gone.

They buried her on the hillside near her home. The grave is unmarked, as most graves are, and no one quite remembers where it is. Or perhaps they would rather not remember. Some memories are just too painful to keep.

Chapter 6

Into the Valley

The Great Rift Valley runs like a giant scar across the face of Africa. Its walls rise steep and high, and its rugged slopes are washed by the rains of a thousand storms. It is a place of exaggerated dimensions, a land of superlatives. Home to the largest, the tallest, and the fastest of all land animals, it also has the longest, the second-largest, and the second-deepest lakes in the world. Here, too, flow the waters of the world's longest river, the Nile—the lifeblood of Egypt and the tears, so they say, of the continent.

The name of the Great Rift Valley is a misleading one, for it is not really a single valley at all, but a series of valleys, enormous country-long valleys rimmed with tall hills and forbidding cliffs. One of these valleys forms part of the border between Zaire and Uganda and passes very near our school at Lukanga. It isn't an area I visit more than three or four times a year, but such is the nature of the land that a visit is rarely forgotten. My weekend at Muhita last year was no exception.

On the morning the trip began, I was in the house packing my bags while Diane did the same for Danny. He was seven now, old enough for his first big safari with his father.

"What time are you planning to leave?" she asked.

"Oh," I said, trying to sound casual, "as soon as I can get off, I guess."

"And what time do you think that will be?" she continued, looking as ever for a little more precision.

"Oh, around two-thirty, I suppose."

"Two-thirty's pretty late, don't you think?"

"Well, yes," I replied, "but you won't believe how much I've got to do before we go."

"Probably not," she agreed, "but tell me anyway."

"Hey," I protested. "I've got my classes to teach. I need to check on the masons, and I promised Kavira I'd stop in at the dorm. Then I've got to take my keys to Masinda and—"

"And play volleyball at one?" she interrupted.

"That too," I admitted.

We take our volleyball seriously at Lukanga, so it's hard to get under way quite as early as one should. But then, I had it on good authority from Tahitya that the trip could be made in three hours. One hour in the car, he said, two hours on foot.

As it turned out, we left at three-thirty, three-thirty on the dot, as I carefully pointed out to Diane, who was there to see us off. It was late enough for her to be a little concerned, but still very good, I thought, considering how much I'd had to do before we left.

"Can we get there before dark?" I asked Tahitya, who was serving as guide for the trip.

"I hope so," he said, "but we'll have to hurry when we leave the car."

"In an hour," I added for reassurance.

"In about an hour," he corrected. "It may take just a little longer."

"You didn't say anything about 'a little longer' when I asked you before," I said.

"No," he agreed, "but we were late getting started, remember?"

I was in no position to argue with the logic, and it was just as well I didn't, for he was right. The ride did take a little longer than an hour—quite a little longer. We didn't park the car until five-forty-five.

"We'll have to hurry," Tahitya said again, as we finally set off on foot, and hurry we did. Danny ran like a veteran down the winding trail, and I followed close at his heels, encouraging him along. When darkness enveloped us around six-thirty, we had already covered a good four miles. But running was impossible now, and we got out the flashlight and picked our way along the narrow path. At eight o'clock, we came to the top of the Great Rift Valley and started gingerly over the edge. At eight-fifteen, the flashlight quit.

The trail which drops into the valley is not a dangerous one as such, for it keeps away from the steepest dropoffs, but it is terribly fatiguing. It is pitted and rough and strewn with debris. Rain-sifted gravel and sand seem almost constantly underfoot, and boulders protrude unexpectedly. Tahitya knew the way by heart and warned us of the major obstacles as we came up to them, but with no light to guide us, we couldn't adjust for the gravel and the ever-present rocks, and we were constantly stumbling.

"Have you ever been over this part at night without a flashlight?" I asked Tahitya, feeling guilty about the worn-out batteries.

"I've never been over it with one," he said.

"Then how do you manage?"

"Usually I make sure I go over it in the daytime," he answered.

"Touché," I thought to myself, but he wasn't trying to win any points and didn't bother to press his advantage.

"I've gone through here plenty of times after dark too," he said. "Sometimes there's a moon to help you along, but often enough it's just about like this."

Lightning flashed in the distance as we stumbled wearily along, and the ominous rumble of thunder echoed low through the empty valley below. I held Danny's hand a little tighter, grateful for the sudden bursts of light, but worried about the chance of rain out here in the open, far from the nearest shelter.

"Ever get caught here in a storm?" I asked.

"Oh yes," said Tahitya. "Once, when I was walking home from Lukanga for the holidays, we didn't get out of class until one, and it took me six hours to reach the end of the road. Then, just before I got to the top where the path starts down, it began to rain. The next thing I knew, the path was so slick and the rain so hard that I couldn't even stand up. I crawled all the rest of the way down on my hands and knees and didn't get in until two in the morning." He paused for a moment and then broke the story off with a quick laugh I've heard so often. "Hah!" he exclaimed. "Now that was a storm!"

There was neither self-pity nor pride in his voice as he spoke, merely a sense of wonderment at the intensity of the storm. Yet as I listened to him talk, it suddenly struck me how little I knew, even now, of the hardships which these people take for granted. I had slept in the same little huts and shared the same food around a smoking fire many times, but I still didn't know what they endured, not really. I might catch a glimpse of it now and again, but for me, there was always a warm bath, a sympathetic ear, and a change of clothes at the end of the trip. For Tahitya and countless others, there were no such comforts. Life was a flip of the coin, they often said, and you couldn't know how it would land, heads or tails, good or bad, but you took what it gave you. You took life as it came, and you didn't complain.

This night, it was in a generous mood. The storm couldn't find where we were hiding, and soon the flashes of lightning faded and were gone. Only the distant rumble of thunder persisted, and again we faced the darkness of the night on its own terms.

The path tipped downward ever more steeply now, and standing became impossible, but even here we were fortunate, for there was grass growing by the path. Tahitya showed the way. He sat down and began slowly descending the slope on the seat of his pants. I took a weary Danny on my shoulders, sat down, and did the same. The trip was turning out to be more than I had bargained for. From the vantage point of our present situation, the afternoon's victory at volleyball somehow didn't seem so significant as it had earlier. Each little bump in the grass made it painfully obvious that we should have left much earlier than we had, and I reflected ruefully that, if life is indeed a heads-or-tails proposition, then it clearly was not our heads we were using.

They say the Lord helps those who help themselves. This may well be, but fortunately for us, He offers help to those who are less deserving too. We knew we needed that help now, and the prayers were going up a lot faster than we were going down—and they weren't long being answered. As we rested in the long grass by the path, uncertain as to how we could go on, we saw high above us the unsteady flickering of a flashlight.

It's not often you can actually watch an answer to prayer as it comes, but that's just what happened that night. We sat, too tired to stand, as the little beam of light came ever closer. Only when the two men who were carrying the flashlight reached us did we manage to struggle to our feet in weary unison.

"*Jambo* [Greetings]," we called, from out of the shadows.

The Bible says some have entertained angels unawares. Certainly the men before us were as welcome as ever any angels could have been, and their timing just as good. But if angels they were, then their disguise was complete. At the sound of our voices, they jumped with surprise and then froze in midstride, unable to go forward or back. I thought for a moment their knees would surely fail to hold them, but they recovered quickly when they saw us and graciously agreed to escort us the rest of the way. Danny was sound asleep by this time, and I carried him the final hour on my shoulders, until we came at last to the narrow ridge of land that was Muhita.

When I woke up the next morning, my whole body was sore, and some parts of my anatomy were sorer than others. But I had come to preach, and I was glad I had. The folks who live in this part of the valley down by the lake call it Buholo—peace—and peace is what I felt that morning. I spent many happy hours visiting with the overflowing crowd at church and later, with many families in their homes, and I left feeling, as I usually do, that I had received far more than I would ever be able to give.

This, for me, is the essence of mission work. What we give is vitally important, for we have a lot to offer and we should be willing to offer it, but what we receive is even more so, and we should be willing to receive it. Buholo—the spirit of peace and sharing—this is what we need to learn. This is what life is about. Many there are in this world who go to bed without food every night, and that is a tragedy, but many others there are who go to bed without compassion, and that is a tragedy no less.

This is the other Rift Valley, perhaps the greatest Rift Valley of them all, and it runs like a giant scar across the hearts of men. Only with the sense of peace that comes from belonging to one great family will it ever be crossed.

We climbed back out of the valley the following morning. It wasn't easy, but it felt a lot better coming out than it had going in. I haven't been back since, but I think of it often. From the fields across the road, you can almost see it. It's just back beyond those hills. The Great Rift Valley. It's a lot closer to home than you may think.

Chapter 7

Triumph and Tragedy

Death is a frequent visitor to these parts of the world—far, far too frequent a visitor. Her cold shadow leaves a permanent edge of darkness where it falls—and few are the homes where it hasn't. Her appearance has come to be expected, yet it is always a shock. Like a lioness at a watering hole, she seems to strike when we are taking life in the largest draughts, enjoying it to the full. And when she moves on, she leaves us wary, conscious as never before of the beauty of life, but looking back with nervous glance, wondering when she will strike again.

One sunny day in the early part of summer, three travelers showed up unexpectedly at our doorstep. There is a photo in our album that shows them standing by their pickup in front of the house, arms around one another and smiles on their faces. When I snapped that picture, death was the farthest thing from my mind. Yet within a month, one of them would be dead.

They were South Africans, and they had already accomplished the near impossible. They had driven across the interior of Zaire, from Lubumbashi to Goma, in six grueling days. No one else I know has made the trip, but to have made it in six days was nothing short of phenomenal. Especially for Joe, Clinton, and Hugh.

The three men were unlikely adventurers. Joe was a portly encyclopedia salesman in his midfifties, Clinton was a young lawyer who had never been out of South Africa, and Hugh was a white-bearded health lecturer, seventy-four years old and barely five feet tall. Unlikely adventurers indeed, yet each man possessed qualities which made the trip seem not only possible, but necessary.

I was meeting Clinton and Hugh for the first time. Joe Birkenstock I had met the summer before.

I had been asked to hold an evangelistic meeting at a village called Kabali, far from the beaten path, somewhere in the back country where Zaire and Rwanda meet. Diane would have come along, but she was expecting someone and decided to stay home while I went on with Danny and Heather.

All day long, we traveled over roads which worked their way cautiously through the hills, roads that advanced and retreated, making great gains, then doubling back as if expecting to meet an unseen foe at any minute. But our only foe was the sun as it raced across a cloudless sky, dodging behind hills and trees, emerging first to our left and then to our right, now in front and now directly behind. It lingered on until we closed to within a few miles of our goal. Then it tired of the race and, with a last convulsive leap, dropped behind a towering hill and stayed out of sight.

Night had fallen. As we neared Kabali, the shadows became long, grotesque fingers, reaching out in silence to place the heavy mantle of darkness securely on our shoulders. We were walking now, picking our way cautiously along the path. Then, suddenly, from out of the darkness came a beam of light and from out of the silence, a voice. An English voice. It was Joe.

I soon learned that Joe had been a missionary in this region many years before and now, fulfilling a lifelong dream, he had come back to reestablish old friendships and to see firsthand the results of the pioneering work he and others had begun. Asked at the last minute by the local elders to help with the upcoming meetings, he knew that I was due to arrive at any time and had come looking for me. But I had been told nothing about his arrival, and his sudden appearance was a complete surprise. Thinking back now to our first encounter, there in the dark forests of Kabali, I always picture one of us uttering those immortal words: "Dr. Livingstone, I presume?" My memory is probably faulty, but it certainly would have been appropriate.

We held the first meeting the following morning. Facilities were limited, and I ended up sharing a chair with Joe. I sat while he spoke in Kinyarwanda. Then he sat while I spoke in Swahili. He had his accordion with him, and we worked it out so that he would play a final selection as soon as I finished. I came to the end of my prepared text and stepped back to change places with him as we had planned. But he didn't move. Instead, he leaned forward and told me to keep on preaching.

"But I've finished my sermon," I said.

"You can't stop now," he insisted. "You haven't had an altar call yet."

"An altar call?" For a moment I looked at him blankly. I'm not an evangelist. I'm a teacher. I've had my share of preaching assignments since I came to Zaire and I've enjoyed them, but it's not something at which I've ever felt overly competent—I certainly had no idea then of how to make an effective altar call. But Joe was occupying the chair and showed no signs of moving, the church elders beside him were nodding their heads approvingly, and the people were waiting. I decided to give it a try.

I spoke for five minutes or so, and Joe played his accordion softly in the background. My presentation was awkward, embarrassingly awkward, but at least it was sincere. I wanted nothing more than for those precious people on the hillside to have the peace that comes from knowing Christ. Dozens of them came forward, and as the deacons and elders took their names for further counseling, I thanked God in my heart for seasoned missionaries who knew what to do and when to do it.

That had been the previous year. Now Joe was back with two friends and a gift—the pickup in which they had come would be left with our mission in Nyamitaba.

I marveled at the stories Joe told me about life in the old days—about elephants crashing through the mission compound, about safaris that lasted for months. And I marveled at his traveling companions. In spite of his seventy-four years, Hugh was all energy and motion. Several years earlier, he had set a record as the oldest man ever to climb beyond 19,000 feet on Mount Everest, and for years he had been touring the world giving health lectures. His schedule book was half filled with appointments and plans for years into the future, and he was eagerly looking forward to climbing the nearby Ruwenzori Mountains. This was his purpose in coming to Zaire. He had set out almost fifteen years earlier to climb these so-called Mountains of the Moon, but there had been a snag in the plans and the climb had been canceled. Now, as a much older man, he was ready to erase what he considered to be a "blot" on his record.

"I was just a kid back then, anyway," he delighted in telling us. "Now I'm in much better shape for the climb."

Clinton was the third member of the party. He was a quiet, considerate man, and very anxious not to be putting anyone to extra work. Though only in his thirties, he wasn't as robust as his traveling companions and found the trip more wearying. A lawyer from Johannesburg and a bachelor, he was intensely interested in people and spent all his spare time visiting at the local market and walking up and down the many paths near our home. He and Hugh would be climbing the Ruwenzoris together while Joe held a series of meetings nearby.

Clinton and Hugh set out from our mission for the mountains in high spirits. They came back ten days later in even higher spirits. They had been successful. Hugh had evened an old score with the mountain, and Clinton had discovered, high in those cloud-shrouded strongholds, a way of life and adventure he had never known before.

But time was running short. The adventure was almost over. The pickup was driven to Nyamitaba, where it was officially presented to the mission, and the three men began planning their separate journeys home. They made arrangements to get together and compare notes back in Johannesburg. But it wasn't to be. Hard on the heels of triumph came tragedy. Tragedy in the form of blackwater fever.

Blackwater fever is a strain of malaria that attacks the brain. It is said to be fatal in as many as half the known cases. Combine it with hepatitis and the chances for survival are slim indeed. Too slim for a body fatigued by the rigors of a thousand miles of bad roads. Too slim for a body worn out by an arduous climb through the highest mountain range in Africa. Too slim for one of the most likable lawyers in Johannesburg. Too slim for Clinton.

He had decided to remain in Zaire much longer than the other two. He spent an extra week at our home and then another month traveling through the interior. No one knows exactly what his itinerary was, but when he finally stumbled out of the bush near Songa Hospital, weary and weak, it was obvious that something had gone wrong, seriously wrong.

He stayed briefly at Songa and then was rushed by mission plane to the better facilities at Lubumbashi. Milton Glovatsky, the pilot, brought him to the hospital and stayed at his side until the end, but there was nothing either he or the doctors could do. Within hours, Clinton was dead.

Clinton died as he had lived, quietly, just a few short miles from where his last incredible adventure had begun. He was a stranger in the land, but his is the story of so many others. A life of potential cut short. A dream unfulfilled. A chapter begun and never finished. . . .

Chapter 8

Little Links and Ketchup

"Don't drop it, Danny," I said.

"Don't worry, Daddy. I won't."

Danny marched proudly down the sidewalk, clutching the precious bottle of ketchup in his hands. I marched right behind, matching him step for step, my eyes on the bottle.

That was no ordinary bottle of ketchup. It had been specially ordered months before. It had been flown a thousand miles by air. It had been bounced over rough mountain roads in a Land Rover and hand delivered by the pilot. And now it was here. At last it had arrived. Ketchup! The very thought was enough to set my mouth watering. For the first time since coming to Zaire, we would be tasting that all-American, all-Canadian flavor again. Tonight we would be celebrating in style. Diane had made french fries just for the occasion, and in a few more minutes the festivities would begin.

I don't know why I suddenly developed such strong feelings for ketchup while we were living at Lukanga. I don't recall ever having such a desire in the past, but there it was. I suspect it was a cultural thing. Nothing says North America more than ketchup does, and I guess that subconciously I wanted that little link with home and my former way of living that the bottle of ketchup seemed to represent.

My big chance came when Bob Roberts was scheduled to make a flight to Nairobi. Bob is our mission pilot and spends much of his time easing his plane in and out of grass strips that masquerade (unconvincingly) as landing fields. The only mowing some of these fields ever get is from his propeller, and the only radar system around belongs to the bats. It was only natural, then, under such circumstances, that Bob was excited at the chance to get away to Nairobi. For him, Nairobi meant luxury. It meant paved strips and navigational aids. It meant fuel at the pumps and spare parts in the stores. For me, it meant *ketchup*.

When we first were asked to come to Lukanga, we had a lot of questions about the isolation and the difficulty of getting food.

"You'll be surprised," we were told, "when the mission plane makes its flight to Nairobi every month. You can get almost everything you want. It'll be practically like living in the big city itself."

They were right. We will be pleasantly surprised when the mission plane makes its flight to Nairobi every month. So far, in five years and more, it's gone four times. Space has always been limited and grocery shopping largely symbolic. Still, we're eternal optimists, and when we heard that another flight had been scheduled, I immediately talked to the pilot and put in my order for ketchup.

The flight was delayed for months, as flights often are. Every time Bob would get all the overflight clearances and landing privileges arranged, his schedule would be changed and he'd be sent someplace else. But finally the big flight did take place, and when he left, Bob promised to do his best for us. He was as good as his word. Ten days after flying out, he returned with the ketchup. There were a few other minor items on the plane, of course: mail from the States, school supplies, the business manager, and things like that, but we had eyes only for the ketchup. Never before had a little glass bottle looked quite so good.

Danny was even more excited that I was. He asked eagerly if he could carry the bottle to the house. I handed it to him with much care and many cautions about holding on tightly, but even as I was warning him, I could see Diane raising her eyebrows dubiously.

"Are you sure—?" she began.

"He'll be careful," I said, trying to express a confidence I didn't feel. "And besides, just look at him. Look how excited he is. It's his moment too. Let him enjoy it."

Against her better judgment, Diane agreed, but whether or not he enjoyed it, I couldn't say. I don't know if he had time. He carried the bottle safely for all of ten yards—and then, before I could react, it slipped cleanly from his grasp! It fell with a sickening crash, and I watched as the thick red liquid oozed over the unyielding concrete.

There is very little on this earth which is more wonderful that the relationship between parent and child. There is also very little which can be more frustrating. I don't know whether God gives us children to make us old before our time or to keep us young forever; to make us wise beyond our years or to help us laugh at our own follies. I suspect it's a bit of each. I certainly hope so. I have only on rare occasions been accused of wisdom beyond my years, and this day wasn't one of them. Danny and I cleaned up the mess in such silence as the circumstances permitted, and our celebrations that evening were subdued.

Several months later, my sister Janet sent me a letter, I don't know whether someone had written home about the ketchup incident or whether it was just a sister's intuition, but she had taken it upon herself to restore that little link with home that I had been wanting so badly. Inside the folds of the letter, she had slipped one of those tiny packets of ketchup that you get at the fast-food places.

It was a thoughtful gesture, a very thoughtful gesture, and if things had worked out, I know I would have appreciated it for what it was. But things didn't work out that way. Unfortunately, she hadn't taken the automatic mail sorters at the post office into her reckoning. I'm not sure whether it was the folding or the spindling, or whether it received some "special handling" but the day we received the envelope has gone down in our family history as "red letter day."

The contents of the envelope were a congealed mass of soggy pulp. Only the address on the outside of the envelope was legible. Mold was growing around the edges and there was no telling *what* was growing inside. The distinctive aroma of ketchup was mingled with an assortment of putrifying odors that rankled in my nostrils for hours. I never did find the courage to open the thing.

Yet we didn't need to. It had served its purpose and somehow after that episode ketchup never seemed quite so necessary again.

Chapter 9

The List

It was known quite simply as "The List" and for twenty-four hours, no one at Lukanga thought about anything else. It was the topic of every conversation, the subject of every debate. From the hangers-on and the passers-by in front of Mayele's store to the cooks in the kitchen, everyone had his own version of—the list. And Khamabu's name was on almost all of them. It came as no surprise, then, to see him looking so glum when I met him on my way back from the boys' dorm.

"Khamabu," I asked, "what's the problem?"

"I'm on the list," he said despondently. "Everybody says so. I'm the only name they can agree on."

"Nonsense," I said. "We don't even have the list yet. We won't know until radio time tomorrow."

"Doesn't make any difference," he said, without looking up. "I'm on it. I'm on the list."

I left him sitting on a grassy knoll by the sidewalk, pulling absent-mindedly at the weeds, totally preoccupied with the list. He would think of nothing else all day, I knew—and probably all night as well. I could hardly blame him. So far, the various lists going around were nothing but guesswork, but the real list would make all the difference in the world to Khamabu, and to many others as well, for it contained the names of those who had failed the state exams.

It was that time of the year again. List time. Results time. Every year in mid-July, our grade twelve students write their state exams. This is a grueling four-day process and is followed by a wait of from two to three months before the results are published in the Kinshasa newspapers. That's where the morning radio schedule comes in.

Each morning at 6:30, the different mission stations around the country talk with one another by ham radio. When Pastor Kalume in Kinshasa gets a copy of the results in one of these newspapers, he relays them to us during the morning schedule. If reception is clear, we can get the names and the percentages copied down in a matter of minutes, but if reception is poor, things can be complicated. That morning, as usual, reception became progressively worse.

"Seven Five, Seven Five," Pastor Kalume called. "Do you copy Seven Eight?"

"Roger, Roger," I answered. "Go ahead, Seven Eight."

"We have the exam results. We have the exam results. Do you copy?"

"Roger, Roger. We copy. How many passed? How many passed?"

Things were going along remarkably well, so far, but now they took a turn for the worse, and I could only make out the words "at Lukanga" before the pastor's voice dissolved in a sea of static. There was a pause, then a confused roar like the crashing of waves on a rocky coast. I deciphered the last great crashing sound as a "twenty-seven" and looked around the room for confirmation, but nobody else had heard it.

The radio room is usually off-limits, but we had made an exception because of the expected announcement, and I was hemmed in by hopeful students and teachers. They were craning their heads this way and that in an effort to keep a clear field of vision to the radio, as if this would make it easier to hear what was being said, and as I leaned back to the radio again, I could see the whole room leaning with me. This time I dispensed with the preliminaries and fairly shouted into the microphone. "Did you say twenty-seven, Pastor? Twenty-seven?"

An agonizing minute went by before his voice broke through the static again. "Negative copy. Negative copy," he was saying.

I repeated my question, and for a brief moment his voice came through as clear as a bell. "Roger, Roger," he replied. "Twenty-seven. Twenty-seven."

A mighty cheer went up around me. Twenty-seven students out of thirty-three was an excellent result, the best Lukanga had ever known. Several years earlier, the day before I first arrived at Lukanga, in fact, the radio had brought a very different message. Only one student in a class of thirty had passed that year. The following year, seven had made it, and the year after that, twelve. So twenty-seven was certainly cause for cheering. But I needed names. Who had made it and who had not? I motioned for silence, and we all leaned to the radio again.

"Seven Eight. Seven Eight," I called. "What are the names? What are the names?"

Nothing.

"Seven Eight. Seven Eight," I called again. "What are the names?"

Again there was nothing. Only the maddening sounds of static came back in response.

They say a drowning man breaks through the surface three times. The pastor's voice had already broken through the static that many times and more, but now it was drowned out for good. I tried for another fifteen minutes, but he had disappeared without a trace. He would be on again early the next morning, I knew, but for today it was all over. All over, that is, but the guessing.

The state exams have always caused a lot of guessing at Lukanga. All too often, it has been second-guessing as we tried to figure out what had gone wrong. Some years, the reason for our poor showing was obvious. The exam schedule would run from Wednesday to Saturday, with several of the most important tests coming on the Sabbath. Our students have always had the courage and the faith to refuse in virtual unanimity to write any Sabbath exams, and a great many of them have given up a year of schooling and a diploma because of it. Yet this was only a partial explanation, for even during years when there were no Sabbath exams, scores were lower than they should have been.

Then I discovered a surprising statistic. For almost every year since our school has been open, the more missionaries teaching at the school, the lower the rate of success on the state exams. At first, I had a hard time believing this, for almost without exception the missionaries had more training and a higher academic degree than the Zairian teachers, yet the figures were very clear. This didn't mean the missionaries weren't good teachers, of course. The majority of them were. It didn't even mean they were the cause of the problem. It just meant there was some connection, and the more I thought about it, the more sense it made.

During my first year at Lukanga, nine different missionaries taught at the secondary school. Two arrived late (including myself), two left early, and another was constantly gone to committees. Here was part of the problem, but it went much deeper than this. Different cultures, different learning styles, different languages, all of these took their toll.

I am a firm believer in missions and the work that missionaries can do. I wouldn't be one if I didn't. I believe we could use far more missionaries than we presently have, and I hope to see the day when we have them. But I don't believe in packing them in great numbers onto one or two compounds. I believe in spreading them around. The missionary's role is that of consultant and catalyst, not of competitor for local jobs.

We scoured the country for the most competent Zairian teachers and staff we could find. Gad Mwangacucu and the Mbyirukira family joined Masinda and the other teachers already on staff, and along with Lisebie Luchman, a missionary from Mauritius, they formed a professional cadre which would rival any school staff anywhere. Katsyoto took over as secretary, and new missionaries coming in were used where they were more badly needed. Some went to the new technical school that was established at Lukanga, but others went to open work in areas the church had never reached before. In three years, we went from eight or nine teaching missionaries to two.

There was a little more to it than that, of course. The missionaries had been living on one side of the campus and the Zairians on the other. That was quickly changed. There were also a few cosmetic changes. We mowed a few lawns, painted a few walls, and laid a few bricks. Morale went up, grades went up, and now here was the result. Twenty-seven out of thirty-three. Or so we thought.

I went down to the radio room early in the morning to get the names of those who had passed and to put an end to the speculation about who had failed. To make sure I could hear properly, I had everyone else stay outside the radio room this time, but the precaution was unnecessary. Pastor Kalume's voice came through loud and clear.

"Seven Five. Seven Five. Do you copy Seven Eight?"

"Roger, Roger," I said. "Go ahead."

"I think you misunderstood me yesterday morning," he said. "I was telling you that at Nyamitaba, thirteen passed out of twenty-seven. Did you copy the number who passed at Lukanga?"

For a moment, my heart sank. Then we didn't have twenty-seven passes at Lukanga. "How many?" I asked, almost afraid to hear the answer.

"Everyone," he said without hesitating. "Everyone. They all passed. Thirty-three out of thirty-three."

He quickly read me the passing percentages, and I scribbled them down. Then I signed off and stepped outside where everyone was waiting, some with their six-name lists in their hands.

"Put away your lists," I said. "You won't be needing them. Everybody passed."

There was a moment's silence, then a resounding cheer which must have lasted half the morning. There was more hugging and laughing than I ever would have thought possible. Messengers raced off in all directions to bring the news to anxious families in nearby villages, and there was a general hullabaloo all day such as can scarcely be imagined.

I didn't find Khamabu until almost noon. He had stayed home in despair and didn't learn the good news until one of his friends finally tracked him down. But his score had been one of the highest—enough to win a scholarship to the university.

"Congratulations, Khamabu," I said. "I knew you could do it."

His eyes glistened, and for a moment he fought for control. "Thanks," he said at length, his voice trembling with emotion. "Thanks for everything."

"Don't thank me," I said. "This is your day, your diploma. You did it."

"No," he corrected, "not by myself. We did it together."

I looked at him standing there, eagerly awaiting a future which only yesterday had seemed impossible, and my thoughts went to Lisebie and Katsyoto, Masinda and Gad Mwangacucu, and all the others who had worked so hard and so long for the success of these students. "You're right," I said. "So very right. We did it together."

Chapter 10

In Hiding

Sprinting across the lawn, I tore off my jacket and threw it aside. It was too visible, too bright. I ran past the avocado trees, across the driveway, and dove into the tall grass by the hedge. Here at least was partial concealment, temporary refuge. Heart pounding from the exertion, I pressed my body flat to the ground and pondered my next move.

My position was far from ideal. I couldn't be seen from the house because of the tall grass, or from the sidewalk because of the hedge, but to anyone approaching from the road and up the driveway, I was all too plainly visible. The more I thought about it, the more I knew I would have to move. But no, it was already too late. Just as I was tensing my muscles and flexing my legs, preparing to run, the situation took a sudden turn for the worse. I heard voices.

Peering out carefully between the long grasses, I spotted two official-looking men standing on the front lawn. They were talking to Renée, our housegirl, who does the thousand and one chores that we never seem to find time to do. This day had been set aside for baking bread, and as the men approached, she had been stepping outside to winnow the wheat. From my hiding place, I could see the flat winnowing basket she was carrying, and I could hear her voice.

"No," she said firmly, as she tossed the grain expertly into the air, "I don't know where he is," and she probably didn't know—exactly. I sighed with relief. Faithful Renée.

As I watched, I could see the men looking around, pointing

this way and that. I couldn't hear what they were saying now, but judging from their gestures, I imagined that they were discussing my whereabouts. If they had come but a scant ten minutes earlier, they would have found me in my office. It was, after all, only a few minutes after eleven o'clock on a beautiful weekday morning. Summer vacation was almost over, and I had slipped away from the office at the school for a quick game of hide-and-seek with Heather and Danny and a few of their friends. And I was having a hard time getting away with it.

I wouldn't really have minded giving up the game and going back up to the office with the two callers. As a matter of fact, I would have been more than happy, for the ants had found me and were making my existence miserable, climbing inside my clothes and biting ferociously.

I recognized the two men who had come to see me. They were from Butembo. But, under the circumstances, I didn't know how to go about making my presence known. Rising to my feet all covered with ants and dirt somehow lacked the dignity expected of the principal of a school. What words could I use to explain to visitors why I was lying flat on my face in the weeds in front of my house? It was hard enough to explain to my wife. No, I would just have to stay where I was and hope for the best.

At last the two men walked away from the house—slowly. If only they would go on the sidewalk, I thought, then they would never see me. As soon as they disappeared behind the hedge, I could slip into the house, change my clothes, retrieve my jacket, and catch up with them by the time they got to the school.

Instead, they decided to go on the road! They walked right past the patch of tall grass where I was hiding. I held my breath. I was sure they would discover me. They had only to turn around and there I was. They couldn't help but see me. But, fortunately, they didn't turn around. They kept on walking, eyes straight ahead. I didn't dare raise my head to see how far down the road they had gotten.

Suddenly Danny came bursting around the corner. I had forgotten about him. "I see you, Daddy!" he shouted, running back and pointing. "I see you! One, two, three on Daddy!"

For a moment I didn't move. Then, gathering up what shreds of dignity I could muster, I rose slowly to my feet and turned, expecting to see the men. I was sure they would hear Danny and look back. But they didn't. I wiped my forehead with relief and gathered up my jacket. That had been a close one.

Five minutes later, I caught up with the visitors outside my office.

"You're a hard man to find," they told me.

"Well," I answered guiltily, brushing a piece of grass from my jacket, "I've had a lot of running around to do recently."

I had a good idea why the men had come. The school year was about to begin, and a great many parents had been coming to Lukanga in an effort to enroll their children. Enrollment is by no means an automatic process, because for every place available, there are four or five qualified applicants. To make things as fair as possible, we have an admissions committee to rule on the merits of each application and to make the final decision. I would explain this in due time to my visitors, of course, but first we would have to go through a delicate process of negotiations. I invited them into my office.

One of the men, the one I knew best, acted as spokesman. He chose his words with extreme care. *"Monsieur le préfet,"* he intoned, speaking first in French to put the conversation on a professional level, between equals, "let me congratulate you on the success of your school. All of Butembo has heard of your success on the state exams."

"Thank you," I said. "Our students worked hard last year."

We spoke for a few minutes more in French. Then the tone of the conversation shifted as he searched for just the proper words with which to state the purpose for which they had come. There was a long pause; then he pulled his chair up close to mine, leaned forward, and spoke confidentially in Swahili.

"My friend," he started, "I have a little problem." He paused again, waiting for my reaction.

"Oh?" I said, noncommittally.

"Yes," he continued, "my colleague here has a son." Another pause. He was hesitant to state his mission forthrightly, I knew, until he had some idea of what kind of an answer I might give, and he waited now for me to follow up on his cue.

"What grade is the boy in?" I asked, obligingly.

"Grade ten," he responded quickly.

"Do you have his school records with you?" I continued.

He was already pulling them out of a briefcase. "They're all here and all are in order," he assured me.

I looked them over quickly and explained our school's policy on admissions. I told him I'd put the boy's name on the list, along with everybody else's, and we'd let him know in a few days whether or not he had been accepted. Now the boy's father spoke for the first time.

"He's a good boy," he chimed in, "and if he ever gives you any trouble, you just let me know and I'll straighten him out." He spoke as if his son had already been admitted. This is a common negotiating technique. Parents anxious to enroll a child are always hoping that somehow they can get the principal to commit himself, or at least give them something they can use for future bargaining in the event the application is refused. I sighed, explained the admissions procedure again, and thanked the man for his offer of cooperation.

Apparently satisfied with the interview, the two men rose and made ready to leave. I accompanied them out the door and down the sidewalk to where they had left their car. Again the conversation switched to French, as if they wanted to leave things on the same solid professional basis with which we had begun.

"Monsieur," began the spokesman.

"Yes?" I asked, self-consciously, removing a twig that remained lodged in my hair.

"What impresses us most about your school," he continued, turning to face me as he spoke, "is that there's no fooling around here. This is one place where people take things seriously."

I looked down the road behind him toward my house. Danny was racing around the corner, looking feverishly for a hiding place. Heather was in the front, counting to a hundred, and various neighborhood children were scampering over the lawn and through the hedge. They were expecting me back at any minute.

I turned to my visitors once again and reached out to shake their hands. "Thank you," I said. "We do our best. And now if you'll excuse me, please. I've got to run."

Chapter 11

A Bag of Cement

I don't like shopping. I never have. There is something in the look of a storekeeper and the way he stacks his goods that makes me positively nervous. I no sooner enter a store than I feel I have somehow stumbled into hostile territory, and I never feel at ease again until I'm back in the open air. But when our business manager left on furlough and the school board in its inscrutable wisdom gave me his job for the three months he'd be gone, I decided to face it bravely and to do it as best I could.

First came the problem of bookkeeping. This was easily solved. I took a large notebook and lined it in columns, the most important of which read "In" and "Out." I toyed with the notion of labeling them "Debit" and "Credit," but this seemed unnecessarily pretentious since I couldn't remember which was which. I wrote "Cash Account Notebook" on the cover in the best modern bookkeeping style, and I set off for town.

I had a long list of things to buy for the school, and just before I left, someone asked me to pick up a bag of cement. I decided to get this out of the way first and went directly to the store that handles cement. It was strictly a one-product store, and the floors were covered with the gritty powder. When I stepped inside, a salesman came over at once.

"Greetings," he said, rubbing his hands together in anticipation.

"Greetings," I responded, looking carefully at the bags of cement along the wall with what I hoped was a knowledgeable manner.

He waited discreetly at a distance while I finished my inspection. Knowing that he was watching, I felt compelled to make a thorough job of it. I punched at a few of the sacks in much the same way that you kick at the tires of a car. Then I scooped up a handful of cement from the floor and sifted it thoughtfully between my fingers.

"Can I help you?" he asked, when I finished.

"Yes," I answered gravely, "I'd like to make a purchase."

"Excellent," he replied, pulling out a pad of invoices and a pen. "Excellent. And what would you like?"

"Cement," I said. "I've come to buy cement."

He said nothing, but looked at me with such a pitying expression that I felt obliged to go on. "But only if the price is right," I added hastily.

I hadn't intended to quibble over the price, since I was only buying a single bag, but my answer seemed decidedly inadequate without some sort of explanation, and on the spur of the moment, I could think of nothing better.

"Three hundred zaires," he said. "That's the price."

"Three hundred," I repeated slowly, as if wondering whether to accept.

By now, as I later realized, he had come to the conclusion that I was planning a major purchase and evidently felt that the situation was becoming more than he could handle alone.

"I'll get the owner," he said.

The owner was a portly, well-dressed man with an aura of importance about him. Somehow he seemed out of place among the bags of cement in the dusty aisles of the store. He motioned me down the hall to a paneled room that served as his office.

"What can I do for you?" he asked when we both were seated comfortably in large leather chairs.

I stated my business at once. "Do you offer discounts?" I asked, "for purchases in bulk?"

I had no more intention of saying "in bulk" than I had of arguing over the price in the first place, but the words just seemed to slip out on their own and there was no stopping them.

"How large a purchase do you intend to make?" he asked, with considerable interest.

I paused, suddenly aware of his mounting expectations. "An entire bag," I said bravely, as if to astonish him (and here I seemed to be succeeding). "An entire bag now and more in the future if the first proves satisfactory."

He seemed at a loss for words and said nothing for an unnaturally long period of time. He looked at me curiously, as if to ponder the meaning of it all, then motioned conspiratorially for me to come closer. I leaned forward across the desk, feeling distinctly uncomfortable. He leaned towards me, his voice dropping to a whisper.

"No discount," he said.

I rose at once and prepared to leave. "Then I shall have to take my business elsewhere," I said, with an air of finality as if nothing could persuade me to change my mind.

He seemed to sense the hopelessness of the situation and said nothing, but I could see his lower lip quivering with emotion as I left the room. I hurried down the hallway, past the waiting salesman, and out the front door. A great sense of relief flooded over me as I reached the street once again. Recovering somewhat, I spent the rest of the day shopping, buying only those items that were down on my list.

Late in the afternoon, purely by accident, I again found myself directly in front of the cement store. Scarcely had I remarked upon this than I was horrified to see the owner coming along the sidewalk towards me. There was no way to avoid him, and I smiled a perfunctory greeting as we passed, hoping he had forgotten who I was.

There was no chance. He was still unaccountably preoccupied with the morning's encounter and asked me at once: "Did you really mean what you said about taking your business elsewhere?"

"Absolutely," I replied, putting on a bold front, although secretly I was pleased to find he was having second thoughts.

He appeared to be profoundly moved. He reached out and

shook my hand with genuine feeling. "Thank you," he said.

A short time later I found another bag of cement in a little store down the street that sold everything from paint to perfume. The bag cost me ten zaires more than I would have had to pay at the wholesale store, but when the salesman told me the price, I paid it at once without uttering a word. Somehow it just didn't seem proper to argue.

Chapter 12

To Build a Church

The next time I visit the church on the hill at Ngumbe, I'm going to bring a tape measure with me—not to measure the church, but the hill. I learned an important lesson on that hill, and I want to see how long it took me to learn it. I figure it was at least fifty yards.

Visiting churches is one of the bonuses of life in these parts. I love these visits, and I make them just as often as I can. Surely, there is no more thrilling way to spend a Sabbath. Of course, some visits are more thrilling than others.

We had a little construction project going at Ngumbe, and I was anxious to see how the work was progressing. Some of the church members in Canada had raised enough money to help finish this church, and so one Sabbath, when construction was nearly completed, I climbed up the hill to the church to give them some words of encouragement. Afterward, they gave me some words of advice.

"Don't go back the same path you came up," they cautioned me. "It's been raining too much. You'd better take the long way around."

Well, it was true that a gentle rain had been falling for much of the day and the path down the hill was a steep one. Still, I've been up and down many steep paths over the years, and I didn't see any reason why I and the men who were to accompany me should surrender to this particular declivity.

"I'll be careful," I assured them, "but I don't have the time to take the long way around. Why, that's half a mile out of my way!"

The men accompanying me said nothing until we came to the steepest part of the path. Then a spokesman uttered three little words that should have been ample warning of what was to come—"You go first," he said.

I went first. In fact, I went alone. I placed my feet carefully on the rain-slicked surface and took one step downward. Then I took another and another. So far, so good. I stepped forward more confidently now, keeping my body turned sideways to lessen the danger of slipping. But suddenly, as the whole congregation stood watching and waiting expectantly, it happened. I lost my footing. My feet skidded around and pointed straight down the hill. My body spun forward and, with no further warning, I was off.

I am not a downhill skier, but if ever I take up that sport, I shall certainly start with a slope far more gentle than this one. I shall also make a point of wearing something other than a three-piece suit for my debut. Indeed, as I raced down that hill, my feet kept in place by the ruts in the path, it was concern for my suit even more than concern for my bones that inspired my struggle for balance. To hospitals and clinics I could go; to dry cleaners I couldn't.

Somehow, with my arms flailing frantically, I managed to keep on my feet as I raced down the hill. I even held on to my Bible and hymnal. But the worst moment came near the bottom, when the path turned sharply to the left. I knew at the speed I was going that I could never negotiate the corner, so just as I reached it, I leaped with both feet together just as high in the air as I could. I cleared the edge of the rutted path and came down in the grass beside it. Here I careened to a stop, sitting down rather suddenly at the end but none the worse for my ride.

Breathlessly, I struggled to my feet, then turned and looked up. Two long weaving skid marks traced my progress down the hill. And at the top, peering down in amazement, stood the whole congregation. It was an opportunity too good to be wasted.

"Next!" I called. But my exploit had left them entirely unimpressed, and there weren't any takers. Shaking their heads, they turned back the way we'd been coming and took the long way down.

I learned something important that day. I learned to listen to what the local people had to say. And I learned something else. It's fine to be quick on your feet, but it's better to use your head for what it was intended.

The church at Ngumbe isn't the only construction project I've been involved in. When the church members back in Canada raised the money to finish the church at Ngumbe, they raised enough to finish it five times over. To this was added some money entrusted to Carey Carscallen, the principal of the technical school, by some friends. Besides this some of the missionaries added their own money, which occasionally was left over at the end of the month. Put together, these funds amounted to a sizable sum for use in little projects here and there.

At our mission station we follow a standard procedure with all of these church-building projects. It means a lot of sacrifice, but I've never found a church yet that wasn't willing to do it. If the church is to be built of brick, the church members make their own bricks. If the church is to be built of stone, they must bring in the stone. The women of the church at Ngumbe, for instance, carried thousands of stones up a hill almost a mile long, over a period of several years, to construct their church building. Church members also must bring in the rocks for the foundation and the floor, as well as find timbers for the roof. When this has been accomplished, the missionaries scrape up the funds for cement and the roofing. They also pay for the masons, although the church members board them and feed them, to keep the cost to a minimum. A local businessman, Tatasi, has also been extremely involved in the building of churches and has been the prime mover behind more than a dozen of them.

I was visiting the church at Mahikwe one Sabbath, and the pastor and elders talked to me about building a more representative church in their village. Theirs was an old mud and stick structure that had seen better days, and besides, the congregation was growing so rapidly it could no longer fit inside.

"You know the rules," I said. "Make the bricks and bring the rocks and we'll see what can be done."

Carey Carscallen and Eldon Bauer, as well as other missionaries, have helped draw up a set of standard church plans. They have calculated how many bricks each plan will take, how many trusses, and so on. My role in the process has simply been to keep speaking encouraging words and to keep the process moving.

I sat down with the folks from Mahikwe, and they picked out the plan they wanted. It would be a church measuring twelve meters by twenty-six (approximately 40 × 85 feet). We figure a church that size can hold about four hundred people.

We have two brick molds at Lukanga that we send around for making the bricks. We call them brick-making "machines," but in fact, the bricks are merely formed by the machine. It is strictly a hand-labor procedure. You shovel in the dirt, pull down a handle to press it in the mold, and lift out the brick by hand. When the members at Mahikwe first approached me, one of the molds was in use by the congregation at Kanyatsi and the other was in need of repair. By the time the folks at Kanyatsi had finished with theirs and Eldon had found the necessary materials to repair the second one, several months had gone by. But at last the molds were ready, and I sent a messenger off to Mahikwe to let them know. The very next day, a group of men from the church were at my doorstep.

"You'll need about twenty thousand bricks," I told them, "and when you're finished, the folks at Bunyakondomi are waiting."

They promised to work quickly and set off with the heavy molds. A week later, they were back.

"Broken mold," they explained.

Eldon is the expert in these things, and so he patched it up and sent them on their way again. A week or so later, they returned. This time it was the other mold. Again, Eldon made the necessary repairs, and they went back to work.

Several weeks later, Eldon came to the office to see me. "What are they doing at Mahikwe?" he asked. "They're wearing me out. Every week, they show up with fresh repairs to be made. They keep breaking my welds."

I promised to tell them to go easy on the equipment and sent a letter up to the church with someone who was going that way. Within a week, the head elder and one of the deacons had come down to see me.

"We were wondering if we could stop yet," they said.

"How many bricks have you made?"

They told me.

"I'm afraid not," I said when I heard the figure. "You'd better make at least another fifteen thousand."

"All right," they said, with an air of dogged determination. "We'll make another fifteen thousand. But we figured forty thousand would probably be enough."

"Forty thousand!" I exclaimed in stunned amazement. "I thought you said 'four thousand.' "

"*Eyehe* [No]," they said, shaking their heads. "Forty thousand."

"Stop everything," I said, "I'll be there tomorrow to count the bricks myself."

When I arrived at their church the next day, I really questioned the forty thousand figure. Our molds make big bricks, and it was hard to believe they had forty thousand of them. But they did! They showed me the pole lean-tos thatched over with banana leaves where they were keeping them, and I counted the bricks by myself. Forty thousand bricks in two months. No wonder the molds had kept breaking. The men of the church had organized themselves into shifts and had worked around the clock to get the job done. The hole where they had dug the dirt was impressive enough by itself, but when I asked how they had gotten so much done in so short a time, they just shrugged their shoulders.

"You told us to work quickly," they said.

We decided to sell the extra bricks to cut down on the rest of the costs. We waited a few months for the bricks to dry out: then we sent over some masons to build them into kilns. The church members had already chopped a vast pile of firewood, and when the kilns were ready, they fired them up. They started right after sundown one Saturday evening and they stayed there twenty-four hours a day until the following Friday afternoon. It took another month for the bricks to cool down. Then we were ready to build.

And that's how it's done in Zaire. I've been involved in seven or eight similar projects in the last couple of years. Tatasi and others have been involved in far more. Now it's hard to travel more than a few miles around here without seeing a neat little Adventist church on a hill. And the more we build, the more we need, for the church is growing by leaps and bounds. It's a challenge that shows no signs of ending. And I hope it never does.

Chapter 13

It's a Boy!

When Teddy Roy was born, I was thousands of miles away. We had been afraid there might be complications with his birth, and since furlough was coming up, we decided it was wisest for Diane to go back to North America a few months early.

The separation was hard on both of us—much harder than we anticipated. So, a few months after furlough, when it became apparent that there would be another addition to our family, we decided we'd had enough separation. The baby would be born in Zaire.

We never regretted our decision. The months before Jonny was born were special months. We prepared for the delivery together, and when Jonny came, I was there. Right there in the delivery room. And it's a good thing I was.

You see, there were complications when Jonny was born. The delivery was easy enough and things turned out very well in the end, but the room itself was a problem. It was one of the strangest sensations I have ever experienced. Unaccountably, at the very last minute, at the worst possible moment, the delivery room started to spin—slowly at first, and then faster and faster, and I was the first one to notice it.

You could hardly blame the others for not reacting more quickly. The doctor, Gianni Galimberti, was a capable physician and a very dear friend, but he was, after all, understandably preoccupied. As was Jan Roberts. She had come over from Lubero to help with the delivery, and her services were greatly appreciated, but she and the head nurse had no choice but to follow the doctor's instructions. And Diane, well, she had her mind on other things. So it was all up to me and I took control of the situation from the start.

I grabbed the delivery table, to steady it, and I held on tight as things progressed. But then, as luck would have it, something went wrong with the heating system. You wouldn't have thought that a little bush hospital like Kyondo would have such a thing as a heating system, yet evidently it did. For the violent spinning seemed to affect it and without warning, the temperature suddenly shot up. My face flushed red in a flash, and I couldn't help but notice that even Diane was beginning to perspire.

"If only they'd hurry," I thought. "I could still keep things under control, if they'd hurry." I was doggedly gripping the table with both hands by now, and I knew I couldn't hold on much longer.

But wait. There was hope. The baby was coming. The nurses sprang into action, and Gianni held the tiny head in his hands. All around me was bustle and confusion. Things were happening faster and faster. The spinning grew worse and worse. I held on tighter and tried to remain calm.

"It's a boy!" shouted Gianni. "It's a boy!"

There were smiles all around the room and everyone relaxed. But everyone was so intent on the delivery, that even now they failed to see what was happening.

The nurse washed the baby while Gianni and Jan attended to Diane. And all the while the room continued to spin, and the temperature continued to climb.

"The baby!" I thought. "What will this do to the baby?"

He was washed and clean by now and all wrapped up in a blanket. The nurse held him out to me, and I cautiously let go of the table. "Let it spin," I thought. "They will have to fend for themselves. I've got to take care of the baby."

I took him tightly in my arms and rushed for the door. Fresh air. That's what he needed. Pushing the door open, I staggered out into the open courtyard and sat down weakly on a low stone wall. I had made it. The baby was safe.

The courtyard was full of women who had been eagerly waiting to see what would transpire. So delighted were they with the baby that they cheered as I rushed from the room. Some of them were even laughing. I held up the baby for everyone to see and they cheered again. I smiled to myself. These mothers were veterans. They had seen it all before, and they knew what was happening. They knew a man of action when they saw him.

I stepped proudly inside the room where Diane had been staying and sat down shakily in a chair. Used to physical activity as I was, this sort of event could be terribly fatiguing. But it was also immensely satisfying. The baby was crying, but I knew he was out of danger. The spinning had stopped, and the temperature had dropped back to normal.

It was another fifteen minutes before the rest of the crew made it back. I couldn't help but notice that they looked at me differently now, and they smiled as they came into the room—even Diane. She had always wondered how I would do in an emergency like this, and now she knew. I smiled back and sat there proudly, holding the baby in my lap and basking in the glow. It was good to be a father again.

Chapter 14

Keeping Fit

I like to keep in shape physically. The way I see it, staying fit and staying in the mission field have a lot to do with one another, for there are plenty of strange bugs and viruses lurking about. Exercise can't keep them away, and I've collected some remarkable specimens myself to prove it, but it certainly makes them easier to deal with. Besides, what better excuse can I give for disturbing the early-morning peace with my running?

I suspect I would still go running, even if there were no benefits to health. I love the feel of a long-distance run. I love to watch the stars and the planets disappear in the early morning. I love to watch the valleys and the hills as they throw back the cotton-white sheets of early morning mist and wake up to a brand-new day. But if anyone asks me, I tell them I'm running for my health. It's a whole lot easier to explain.

My favorite route is right up the road to Rwese. It's a tough four mile climb, but it winds about through some beautiful countryside—and it's all downhill coming back. Still, there are mornings when it's hard to get up. The cotton-white sheets of home have a certain appeal themselves, and at five o'clock in the morning, they are hard enough to throw back. But even then, it is easy to keep in shape at Lukanga. There is volleyball and soccer and all of the walking you ever could want. And, when you're doing it all at seven thousand feet of altitude, you can't help but feel that you're fit.

And that is why when Kavira, the girls' dean, and Katsyoto,

my secretary, told me they were walking over to the hospital at Kyondo to visit one of our students, I thought, "Why not go along?" Neither of these women is particularly involved in athletics, and since they would be bringing a few baskets of food along with them, I thought they might appreciate someone who was physically fit accompanying them just in case they should need some assistance. And when I learned that Pilipili's mother was coming, I was sure of it. It was the only gentlemanly thing to do.

Pilipili was one of our newer students, and she had been troubled with some sort of mysterious ailment almost from the start of the school year. It was at Kavira's insistence that she had gone to the hospital for tests, and now Kavira felt responsible to see how she was coming along. Since Katsyoto was also the assistant girls' dean, it was only natural that she go along for the visit. As principal, I wanted to keep in touch as well.

Bush hospitals in Zaire aren't like hospitals in North America. Here different wards are in different buildings, separated by open courtyards and separate buildings. Nursing care is limited to giving medication, taking temperatures, and things of that nature. As for food and for any other necessities, those who are able, take care of themselves; those who aren't, bring a family member along.

Pilipili was running out of food. The person who was staying with her had sent back word that more was needed right away. It was Friday—market day—that we got the message. Diane bought some vegetables, and Pilipili's family bought some cassava. Then on Sabbath, immediately following the church service, we prepared to set out on our mission of mercy. The first item of business was to divide the load evenly among us.

Pilipili's mother was a frail-looking woman, bent and deeply wrinkled, yet she took her full share of the load. She was probably around fifty years of age, and possibly younger, because women age quickly in Africa. The constant labor in the fields, the many children they bear, the loads that they carry—all of these take their toll. An African woman's lot in life is a hard one. That's one of our biggest concerns at Lukanga, and it's something the Kaviras, Katsyotos, and Pilipilis are helping to change. But for now, we were in it together, and I slung my sack of cassava over my shoulder and followed behind as Pilipili's mother started up the path to Kyondo.

Kyondo is twenty miles from Lukanga by the road. It is probably just a little over half of that by the paths. When we left, it was early afternoon, and the sack of cassava felt light. By the time we were halfway there, the afternoon was well along and my shoulders were beginning to ache. I was carrying no more than the women, but I was using muscles that hadn't been used in years, and they were beginning to complain. It was Pilipili's mother who noticed the way I was struggling.

"Let me help you," she offered.

I shook my head. *"Eyehe."* I wasn't ready yet to admit that an elderly woman was better at this than I was. It was bad enough to admit that Kavira and Katsyoto were.

We walked along some more, and that sack just grew heavier and heavier. I kept switching it from shoulder to shoulder, but I was clearly out of my element, and I didn't know how much more I could take. And all the while, the women kept up a steady stream of chatter. Most of it was much too quick for me to follow, but there was a lot of giggling going on—I had an idea that some of it was directed my way.

After a while, we stopped for a brief rest. The trip was tiring even for the women, but things were only reaching the crisis stage in my case. Needless to say, I was glad for the breather. Pilipili's mother took advantage of the break to repeat her offer.

"Let me help you," she repeated.

"Eyehe," I insisted. "I can make it."

"Then let me show you how to carry the load," she suggested.

"All right," I agreed, giving in. "Show me how it is done."

She took a short loop of flat rope from her basket. She placed one end around my sack and then, lifting the sack to my back, she put the other end around my forehead.

"Now tip your head forward and put your hands back here," she instructed, showing me how to clasp my hands together behind my head to support my neck. I had seen the women doing this hundreds of times, so I had a fair idea of how it was done, but this was the first time I had ever tried it myself.

The result was astounding. There was no strain on my shoulders whatever, and the weight seemed to be cut in half. I thought at first that my neck muscles would soon start to protest, but it never happened, and I was able to finish the walk to the hospital in relative comfort. I might also add that it didn't hurt that the women slowed the pace just a little over the last leg of the journey. I would like to think it was because they were getting a little tired too, but if so, they showed no other signs of fatigue.

We reached the hospital at five-thirty, and we enjoyed a half-hour visit. Pilipili was doing well and was happy to have some company. She was also happy to have the food. And I, for one, was glad to be rid of it.

The trip home was harder than I thought it would be. The terrain had changed. The hills we'd climbed earlier were shorter going down. The hills we'd gone down were longer going up. And there seemed to be more of them. Some of the longest I was sure I hadn't even seen before, and I was glad I had nothing to carry as I struggled along. Even with a rope around the forehead and hands behind the head, this would have been very slow going. It was slow enough as it was. I don't know what time we got back. I just know it was late, and I was a lot more tired than anyone else seemed to be.

I slept in late the next morning. The stars had long since disappeared by the time I awoke and I was in no shape for running. In fact, it was several days before I felt up to it again. And ever since, when I run, it's with a new sense of humility. I still love the feeling it gives me. I still love to watch the stars as they fade. But for now, no matter how far I run or how fast I go, I can't help but feel that Kavira and Katsyoto are matching me stride for stride. And somehow, just up ahead, I know there's a frail-looking woman of fifty, bent and deeply wrinkled, running the race of her life and showing us how it is done.

Chapter 15

The People of the Forest

To an outsider, the world of the Ituri Forest is a dark and forbidding place, filled with strange noises and wild animals. Water drips constantly from the trees, monkeys scamper overhead, and the great hornbills fly back and forth across the clearings. It's a world set apart, and somehow it all seems completely unreal. Even the trees have an unnatural quality. Many of them have great vines hanging down and great roots soaring up fifteen and twenty feet in the air.

I have entered the Ituri Forest only three or four times and claim no special knowledge of her secrets, no special understanding of her ways. I wish that I could, for the Ituri is a fabulous place, and her secrets are surely worth learning. Yet, for me it always holds a sense of foreboding and gloom. I feel it by day, when the light sifting down through the branches is tired and pale, and I feel it profoundly by night.

The clearing at night seems to shrink. The trees and the noises close in, and the shadows come alive. The bushbaby's cry and the call of the owl are menacing, frightening things, and time seems to slow to a crawl.

But these are an outsider's thoughts, and even an outsider senses that things are very different for the people who live in this forest. The Ituri for them is a friend. It is a part of them, just as surely as they are a part of the forest. These are the Mbuti. They have been called Pygmies by the rest of the world since time immemorial, but one doesn't use the word in their presence. To them it's an insult, a term of derision, for that is the way it has often been used. For centuries, the Mbuti were thought to be something less than human, and even today this notion persists in certain quarters. Perhaps it's their size or the unusual color of their skin or any of the hundreds of meaningless physical features which the outside world uses as a standard by which people are judged. Whatever the reason, it means nothing out here in the forest, where the outsider stumbles and only the Mbuti stand tall.

I have read that the Mbuti have one of the most democratic societies on the face of the earth, and from what I have seen, there is every reason to believe it. There are no chiefs among them. Instead, each village has a *baraza*, round hut built in the center of the clearing. This is their council house, their forum for discussion, the place where decisions are made. There is always a fire burning in the baraza, a smoky, half-hearted sort of fire, and often enough there is a discussion going on or a game being played or a net in the process of repair. It is the nets that stand out in my memory.

I knew very little about the Mbuti the first few times I visited them, and I knew nothing at all about their nets. I have since learned that these are a key element of their hunting style, for they set them up in strategic locations and scare the wild animals into them. I only wish I had taken the trouble to learn this before I made my first visit.

When I entered their village clearing, the women were off to one side stacking up a pile of the *mongongo* leaves, which they use for thatching their roofs. They knew I was coming, for I had sent word ahead, but they cheerfully ignored me as I approached and went on with their work. The men were in the baraza and, unlike the women, they quickly left what they were doing and came over to say hello.

"*Jambo* [greetings]!" I called to them.

"*Karibu* [welcome]," they answered.

I shook hands all around, and they made room for me in the baraza. I got the part of the log directly downwind from the smoke and there I sat, trying not to look terribly uncomfortable and wondering if it would be appropriate to start the conversation. They seemed to be wondering the same thing. There was an awkward silence until Kapita, whom I had met before, cleared his throat and proceeded to speak.

"You are here," he remarked, with an air of great satisfaction.

"Yes," I responded, "I am here."

He nodded his head gravely. "It is well," he said.

"Yes," I agreed, "it is well."

Silence descended again, and the men all went back to their work. They were making what looked like a volleyball net, which I assumed that they used to go fishing. Their string seemed to be exceptionally high quality, and I wondered whether they had gotten it in trade with some of the villagers who lived in that area.

"Where do you buy your string?" I asked Kapita, more to get the conversation started than anything else.

He looked at me and then at the rest of the group, and they all started laughing and talking at once. The conversation had started, all right, and I thought for a while it would never quit. Kapita repeated the question to the man beside him, greatly stressing my use of the word *buy*. He, in turn, passed it on to the next man, and so it went, around the fire, even though they had all heard it perfectly well from the first.

The Mbuti have a marvelous way of laughing until the tears come to their eyes. When they hear a good joke, they like to hold on to it. I just sat there feeling foolish, laughing along with the rest but not quite sure what I'd said. I did have the distinct impression, however, that the string that they used wasn't bought.

After a while, Kapita picked up a length of *nkusu* vine, which was lying in a heap on the ground. "Watch," he said.

I watched. He laid it across his upper leg, then rubbed it quickly back and forth with one hand. This immediately produced the handsome string which I had admired.

They all laughed again at my appreciation of this skill, or perhaps at my ignorance of it, then they set back to work, still exchanging a few comments between them.

I was embarrassed by the poor beginning I had made and decided to atone by asking a more sensible question.

"Tell me," I said, "where do you fish with this net?"

By now they had decided that I was some sort of comedian and hooted with pleasure at my joke. I quickly concluded that the time was not right for conversation and went off to examine their school.

For several years now, our church has been running an experimental project among the Mbuti, about fifteen or twenty kilometers from the town of Njiapanda. They asked us to teach their children to read and to write, and so we have established a tiny elementary school at the edge of the clearing in one of their villages. Kavis was the first teacher, and now each year student missionaries go out from our school at Lukanga to work with the project. Masumbuko is in charge and has developed an agricultural and medical work to go along with the educational side of things.

The work is a very delicate one in many ways. It depends on a few volunteers coming forward each year, and it requires a great sensitivity. A number of the forest people have become baptized members of the Adventist Church, and no one really knows how an Adventist Mbuti should live, because there never has been one before. It is something which only they will be able to show us. No one really knows how they will use their new training, either. Reading and writing have never been part of their culture, but these are skills they are anxious to learn, and, once again, only they can decide what changes this will mean in the way that they live.

As I walked around the school building, examining it with interest, I was a little concerned to find some of the tools we had sent lying around on a table.

"Shouldn't these be put away?" I asked.

"They are put away," someone answered.

"But this building is wide open," I protested. "It doesn't even have windows or doors. These tools aren't safe. Someone might take them."

The thought seemed to surprise them. "Who?" they asked with concern, as if I had received word of an impending robbery.

I realized then that I still had a lot to learn about these people, and during my next few trips to the forest I tried to do just that. I still managed to ask a few questions that provoked great amusement, but I learned to ask questions that gave me some insights as well.

One day near Mount Hoyo, in a different part of the forest, I asked an old Mbuti whether he'd ever seen an elephant killed.

"Six times," he told me. "Six times I was there for an elephant kill, but the last time was many, many years ago."

"How do you do it?" I asked.

"When we find an elephant," he said, "we prepare a powder to blow in its eyes. It may take us days to get close to it, but when we do, we come up to it very very carefully. One man passes in front with the powder in the palm of his hands. When he gets close to the elephant, he blows the powder into its eyes. Then he jumps out of the way, and the elephant starts moving like this."

Here he broke off his story and went into a very lifelike imitation of a blinded elephant swaying angrily back and forth. His arm became the elephant's trunk, and so caught up did he become in the portrayal, that I had to prompt him at last to go on with the story.

"That was my job," he said, "to blow the powder into its eyes. Then another man runs under it with his spear and jabs it like this."

Here he made a series of quick upward thrusts with an imaginary spear.

"He runs right under the elephant?" I asked in astonishment.

"Right under it and out the other side," he answered proudly. "A tall man could never do that!"

"Does anybody ever get hurt?" I continued.

"The second elephant from the last that we killed," he said, "I was in front and my friend was underneath. Then the elephant went like this with his foot."

He gave a stiff-legged kick straight out sideways. "Poof! My friend went through the air, and when he came down he was dead."

"What did you do?" I asked.

"We buried him, and then we followed the elephant until it died."

"But how did you carry the meat back to your village?"

He laughed. "We carried the village to the meat," he said. "We always do. Whenever an elephant is killed, that's where we go to live until most of the meat is gone."

We talked for another half hour about past hunts and past glories, and his eyes misted over as he told of the life he had known. Just an old man and his memories, but they were all he had now, for he no longer had the forest—not really. He was living with several other families in a village near a tourist hotel. They had been brought in by the local government to encourage the tourist trade. There were very few animals in the area, and they were reduced to dancing for the visitors and begging for money.

The last thing he did before we left him was to ask for a teacher for his people who still lived in the forest. It was only with an education, he said, that his people would be able to live the kind of life they wanted. His words sounded very familiar. They made me think at once of our Njiapanda project.

I've been back to the little village in the forest near Njiapanda just once since the school year started up. The building was finished, the doors had been installed, and the tools were still there. Close to thirty young Mbuti were learning to read and to write. They were coming in from all over that part of the Ituri.

I asked young Fungabitu if he liked going to school.

"*Ndiyo,*" he beamed. "Yes indeed."

Then I asked some of the older folks what they thought of the school. They spoke of it with pride and told me that because of it, their children would have chances they themselves never had.

I hope they are right. I hope the Mbuti get those chances. They certainly deserve them, for their lives have been far too short and too hard and too often touched by tragedy. I hope they find a better way, and I think that they can, but I can't help thinking of their love for the forest and the joy that they find in its secrets. I wish them the best for the future, but I hope they never lose what they have.

Chapter 16

A Turning in the Path

They say that the father is always the last to know. And when Teddy Roy was born, they were right. Very right. Folks from Washington state to Nova Scotia were informed of his birth before I was. Ham radio operators on three continents knew all of the intimate details. Only I, his father, was left in the dark; for Teddy Roy was born in Canada on the thirtieth of March, and I only received word of it in Zaire on the eleventh of April.

Jan Roberts told me the big news in the morning, over the mission radio from Lubero. She'd heard it from her father who's a missionary in Rwanda. He got it from someone who got it from a ham radio operator in Michigan. The man in Michigan got it from Diane's aunt, who got it from Diane's parents. And they got it straight from Diane. So it was almost like being there myself.

This is the hard part of life in the mission field– the things that don't happen the way that we'd like. The lines that don't come from the script. And when Teddy Roy was just two years old, the script fell completely apart.

It was a sunny Sunday morning in July—the sort of day when you feel nothing could possibly go wrong. I had just left some visitors at the airstrip in Lubero and was driving with Heather and Danny back over the road to Lukanga.

Road? Perhaps the term is misleading. Loose gravel and hairpin turns. That's more like it. That's what links Lukanga and Lubero—washouts and boulders and mud. It's only a twelve-mile stretch, but it takes forty-five minutes to cover the distance—up over the pass between the two valleys and down the other side. There are so many twists and turns near the top that a passenger can get out of the car and make better progress on a footpath, up and over the crest of the hill and down to the road on the other side. Indeed, for Heather and Danny, this is always the highlight of the trip.

Danny takes it seriously. For him, it's a race, and he's always by the side of the road waiting when I get there with the car. For Heather, it's different. She likes paths far too much to be hurried. She ambles along leisurely, looking for teasel plants to collect or for pieces of quartz or for flowers. As far as she is concerned, the trip over the road is something to be endured just so this moment can be enjoyed. For roads are hard and rough and seem never to go near the most interesting places. Their only concern is to get there. Paths are different. You meet people on paths. You visit the villages. You wander along the little streams and around the big trees, and in the end you get there just the same. That is why for Heather, a road is just a road but a path is a friend.

I left Heather and Danny at the usual place that morning, and when I reached the other side where the path meets the road once again, I was hardly surprised to see that Heather was nowhere in sight. Only Danny was there, a big grin of triumph on his face.

"Where's Heather?" I asked.

"Oh, she's picking some flowers," he said with disgust. "I told her she'd never beat you."

I took Danny's hand, and we walked back the little path together until we found Heather. She was clutching a handful of woebegone weeds, which she proudly presented to me. Then we all turned and walked back to the car together.

We drove on then, around many more curves and turns until we came to the little village of Lukanga. Past the Catholic mission we drove and up the road toward our school. Almost home now. But then, just as we came around the last sweeping turn, someone pulled alongside me and tried to go past.

"Uncle Carey is waving at you," said Danny.

I looked back and slowed down as Carey Carscallen pulled up from behind on his motorcycle.

"You'd better go back to the Catholic mission," he said. "Teddy Roy just grabbed hold of a wire, and his hand's been burned pretty badly. Concetta's taking care of him."

"Where's Diane?" I asked.

"She's up at the house. She's taking it pretty hard."

I turned the car quickly around and hurried back to the Catholic mission, hoping that the news would be good. But it wasn't. I found Teddy Roy sitting quietly on Dorothy Carscallen's lap, and although he showed me his hand with scarcely a whimper, it was clear at once why Diane had taken it so hard. The burns were deep and extensive.

The accident had occurred while Diane was visiting some friends. There is rarely any electricity hooked up to the homes during the day, and seldom enough in the evenings. But this day was an exception, and a makeshift wiring job had left a live wire exposed. Like all of the wiring in Zaire, it was 220. Teddy Roy found it, and when he was alone in the room, he grabbed it with his right hand. The shock threw him to his back on the floor. Diane heard nothing from the next room, but for some reason, she felt impressed to check on him. She found him just able to faintly call, "Mama, Mama," as the current tossed him about. Smoke was coming up from his hand, and the odor of burnt flesh was strong.

She grabbed a piece of firewood and knocked the wire from his hand. Someone sent for the Carscallens, and they had just brought him to Concetta when I arrived on the scene. Concetta dressed the wounds as well as she could and urged us to take him to the hospital at Nyankunde at once. This is a big hospital run by the Africa Inland Mission on the edge of the Ituri Forest. We received permission for an emergency flight, and soon we were bumping over the Lubero road once again. But this time, there was no waiting around at the top, and, before long, we were at the airstrip and in the air.

The rich green colors of the Ituri filled the horizons before us as we flew along. From that height, it looked more like an algae-covered sea than a forest, and the scattered clearings stood out like little islands. A lone cloud sailed lazily past beneath us, and off to the right, a thousand others were moored along the entire chain of the Ruwenzori Mountains.

We flew on for an hour and more, and finally the forest gave way to the grasslands. Buildings and roads appeared as by magic, and we came down at the long, grassy strip by the hospital.

The doctors attended to Teddy Roy's wounds at once. "It's a miracle he's alive," they told us when they heard what had happened. "Had he fallen on his left side, the current would have passed through his heart and very probably killed him."

But he hadn't fallen on his left side. He'd fallen on his right side, and although he will always bear scars on his elbow, where the current passed through, we knew that the doctors were right. A miracle. That was no figure of speech they were using.

After determining that there was no immediate danger from convulsions or from any other complications, the doctors dressed the wounds, but there was very little else they could do.

"He's going to need plastic surgery," they said.

They were hopeful that the surgery could wait for a while, and they sent us back home, hoping for the best as the wounds began to heal. Thanks to Concetta's constant attention, there was no infection, and the burns healed over completely. But Teddy Roy's index finger, his thumb and the palm of his hand remained a mass of scars, and he no longer could use his right hand. As time went by, it began to curl into a tight little ball, and we grew more and more concerned. It was clear that the situation was growing worse. We decided then that only a specialist could give us the answers we needed. Arrangements were made, and Diane took the long trip back to North America with Teddy Roy and Jonny. There she learned that Teddy Roy would need immediate surgery to regain the use of his hand. Not just one operation, but a series. With constant care in between.*

* The operations were successful and Teddy Roy has largely regained use of his hand.

It was late one night that I heard the news, and I hardly knew what to think. For this is my world and I love it. It's where I belong and where I want to be. But the paths of life are seldom as straight and as smooth as we'd like. Loose gravel and hairpin turns. Washouts and boulders and mud. That's how it seems to go a lot of the time, and that's how it was going for us. We'd be back, I knew. We would pass this way again. But for now, we were facing a detour. Like it or not, we had come to a turning in the path.

Chapter 17

Miracles

As soon as I knew for sure that we would be leaving Zaire, I decided to indulge in a little exercise in nostalgia. I would make those last few days special ones, days I would never forget. Once the packing and planning were done, I would walk the old paths one more time, feel the cool breezes blowing down from Rwese, and watch the little children as they played. I would visit all my favorite places again, say goodbye to my friends, and forever fix those familiar fields and faces in my mind.

But it wasn't to be. The last weeks were busy ones, and the last few days even more so. All of my carefully laid plans went for nothing. Yet in those final days and hours, I was to feel again the beauty of this country and to know the warmth of her people even more deeply and more fully than ever I had before. And somehow, in the midst of that last frantic week, when time ran like water through my fingers, God was to give me something which was beyond the reach of time, something which would last forever—a miracle.

Miracles come in all shapes and sizes, I know, but we seem to like the biggest ones best. There is something about the flash of good fortune or the tension of near tragedy that appeals to us. Yet miracles come in small packages too, and like a little gift when it's least expected or a card out of season, it is these which show most clearly the Sender's love.

During our years in Zaire, there were many reminders of God's watchcare, but two in particular stand out. They were little things, yes, even unimportant things, but I knew they were miracles nonetheless. The first occurred during our second year.

I had a Sabbath preaching engagement at a tiny ten-member church not too far from Lukanga. As usual, I was traveling by motorcycle, and, as usual, I was late in getting off. Hoping to make up for lost time, I hurried down the little dirt road as fast as I felt I safely could, but barely had I covered the first kilometer when the engine suddenly coughed and quit. I checked to see what the problem was and found, as usual, that it was my own fault. I had forgotten to put in the gas before I left. I switched the gas line over to the reserve tank and faced an immediate decision: Should I go on or turn back? The reserve tank had a very limited capacity, and I knew it was doubtful whether I could make it there and back again. Still, if I went back now for gas, I'd be late for sure. Figuring that if worse came to worse I could always walk, I decided to press ahead and at least be on time for my appointment.

The church service went well. I had a pleasant visit afterward with the members, ate in one of the homes, and headed back. I started out with a little half-prayer.

"Lord," I said, "You know as well as I do that I should have checked the gas before I left, but I do have another talk to give at three o'clock, and I sure don't feel like pushing this bike all that way."

That was all I said, all I felt I had a right to say under the circumstances, and as I rode along I kept waiting for the engine to quit. Rain was threatening to fall at any time, and I had visions of being soaked to the skin as I pushed the bike along. But it never happened. The rain held off and the engine kept purring beautifully. Until I pulled onto my own driveway, that is. There the purring stopped.

My driveway is about twenty meters (sixty-five feet) long and slopes up a little hill. I ran out of gas just before I started up, and my momentum carried me on to where it flattens out by the house. All I had to do with the bike was park it!

I told my experience to the students at our young people's meeting that afternoon. "Just a little miracle," I said. "I could have walked and perhaps should have, but the Lord brought me home."

They disagreed. One of the grade twelve students stood up. "There are no small miracles," he said. "That God should be interested in the little things of our little lives is a very big thing instead."

Indeed it is. He was right and I knew it, as I was to know it time and again over the years. Yet it was during our final week in Zaire, during the last hectic rush, that I felt it the most.

It was Tuesday, six days before we were scheduled to leave. I had just arrived in Goma to arrange for the shipping of our two crates back to America, and I had fond hopes of getting back to Lukanga with the school truck on Wednesday, or at least by Thursday. There were, after all, only two simple steps required before the goods could be shipped. First, I needed a signed statement from the secret police that the crates had been found to contain no contraband; and second, I needed a customs declaration. In theory, each was at most a half-hour transaction.

I went to the office of the secret police at once. Three guards were sitting outside the building playing cards. Their rifles were leaning against a pillar nearby.

I explained my business. "The boss isn't in," they said.

"When will he be in?"

"Four o'clock."

I was back at three and I stayed until five, when the card game ended and they chased me off the premises. They left me with a parting promise. "He'll be here in the morning at eight—guaranteed."

I arrived in the morning at seven-thirty and the boss showed up—at eleven. He didn't bother to inspect the crates but simply signed the paper and sent me on my way.

I was happy to go. The guards had been pleasant company, but time was beginning to run short. It was Wednesday morning. Thursday would be a holiday, and there was no telling what time the customs office would close for the celebrations. I knew only that it would close early.

I was right. When I arrived at the customs building shortly

before twelve, a guard cheerfully informed me that everything was closed and that everyone was gone "in honor of the holidays." He was kind enough to be apologetic, but there was nothing to be done. I would have to wait until Friday.

This new development complicated matters considerably. I had been hoping to make my little tour on Thursday and Friday, to see all my friends and to say my goodbyes, but now that plan would have to be abandoned. In addition I had scheduled back-to-back sermons at the two Lukanga churches for Sabbath morning. They were to be my farewell sermons, my last chance to meet with the members, and I was determined not to miss them for anything. But Lukanga was three hundred kilometers away, and the school truck does well to average twenty kilometers an hour for the trip.

Friday was not without its frustrations and delays, but it went better than the earlier part of the week. By noon, the final arrangements had been made, and we were on our way at last. The prospects for getting back on time were rapidly diminishing, but I felt at least some of the worry beginning to drain away now that we were on the road. There is nothing harder for me than waiting, and after a full three days of it, even walking would have brought some measure of relief.

The scenery on parts of the Goma-Lukanga trip is beyond description. There is the desolate grandeur of the lava beds and the awesome majesty of the volcanoes. The forests in places have never been touched by the hand of man, and it all seems so unspoiled and beautiful. As we approached the midway mark of our journey, two lionesses crouched by the roadside, oblivious to our passing, and the great herds of antelope watched warily from a distance.

As for me, I was looking warily at my watch. Six o'clock had come and gone, and the main roadblock, just ahead, would be closed for the night. If we got stopped here, there would be no sermons at Lukanga.

When we pulled up, anxiously peering into the night, the guard was still in his little office by the side of the road. He had the keys in his hand and was just locking up. What had caused him to linger an extra half hour I didn't know and I didn't ask, but I thanked him heartily as he graciously opened the gates and allowed us to continue on our way.

Things were beginning to look a lot better by then. There were no more major obstacles ahead of us. There was just one more roadblock, a minor one, and we knew we could talk our way through it. The road was in good shape, and the weather was holding up well. After so many setbacks and delays, after so many frustrations, everything was going our way at last. The night air was cool and refreshing, and all the weariness we had felt disappeared. It seemed too good to be true, too perfect to last—and it was. Two hours later, our trip came to a grinding halt.

They say that the hunter who was spared by the lion was bitten by the rat. So it was with us. We had gotten by the obvious obstacles only to be laid low by the unexpected. One of the mainsprings on our truck broke without warning, shattered beyond repair. It looked like a long wait, and we descended on a nearby Adventist clinic to find a place to spend the night.

The breakdown occurred near the town of Kanyabayonga. Our clinic in that town is run by a male nurse named Barema. Most people, I am sure, would be less than pleased suddenly to find a dozen guests showing up in the late evening, but Barema is not like most people. He was delighted.

I was less so. I wanted to keep moving, and I explained my situation to Barema. "Impossible," he said when I finished. "There won't be another vehicle on the road until morning and even then you won't find them here. They went by here earlier in the evening. The drivers all spend the night in Kayna. That's the only place to catch a ride for Lukanga."

Kayna was twenty kilometers further along. "I guess I'll have to walk to Kayna," I said.

Several of the passengers on the truck volunteered to walk along with me, but Barema's sense of hospitality wouldn't allow it. "Let me see what I can work out," he insisted, and disappeared into the night.

An hour later he was back. "I've found you a ride," he said. A friend of a friend of his had an old car, a vintage Volkswagen, and had agreed to drive me as far as Kayna. I waved a grateful goodbye to Barema, climbed into the car with my two unknown benefactors, and set off again.

Halfway to Kayna, there was a flash of light, and smoke started to pour out from under the dashboard. The driver slammed on the brakes, and the car skidded wildly to a stop. We all jumped out and ran quickly up the road, half expecting some sort of spectacular explosion behind us, but the smoke died down almost as quickly as it had started up. We let a few more minutes go by, and then the two men got cautiously back inside and peered under the dash. Five minutes later, they emerged in triumph.

"Just the wires," they announced.

I'm not sure what wires they were talking about or why they produced so much smoke, but we gave the little car a push, the engine caught, and we were on our way again.

We arrived at Kayna around eleven o'clock. I went at once to the Adventist clinic in that town and knocked on the door where the dispenser lived. His wife and daughter were still up, studying the next day's Sabbath School lesson by the light of a kerosene lamp. They called Kanyamayaga, who dressed hurriedly and came out to visit; then they disappeared into the back of the house.

Kanyamayaga has a beautiful home, part of which doubles as the clinic. The walls are made of sticks and mud, but it is kept fully as clean and as neat as any home in North America and probably better than most. He assured me that there was no point in going on that night, that my only chance of catching a ride was in the morning, and I was more than happy to accept his offer of a room for the night. His wife and daughter, he told me, were getting things ready.

I had expected to be in bed within a few minutes of my arrival, and there was nothing I wanted more. I had been on the go since dawn and was absolutely exhausted. But it seemed that Kanyamayaga wanted to talk and so we talked—on and on for almost an hour. Every now and then, he slipped to the back of the house "to see how things are coming." I couldn't imagine what was taking so long.

The mystery was finally explained when his wife and daughter came back, for they proceeded to fix up the table with a beautiful tablecloth and candlesticks. Then they brought out a full-course meal. They had even prepared french fries! It was a lesson in hospitality that I shall never forget.

After I finished eating, I wished them all farewell, for I would be leaving early and didn't want to disturb them again.

Then I made my way to bed. As I did so, I glanced at my watch. It was exactly midnight.

At five o'clock the following morning, I slipped quietly out of the house. The road was deserted. There wasn't a car or a truck, not a chicken or a goat in sight. Even the skies were empty, for the stars had gone and the sun had not yet arrived.

By five-thirty I was getting some company. The young boys were up first, leading their goats along the road, looking for a suitable patch of weeds where the goats could be tied for the day. Then the women were up, their hair still uncombed, their skirts pulled loosely around them, and their water jugs perched on their heads.

There is a special fraternity among people who get up at this time of the day, and they called out to one another and to me, where an hour or two later we might well have passed by in silence. They asked me where I was going and where I had been, and they argued with one another over my chances for getting a ride. But I still hadn't seen a single vehicle on the road, and I had been walking for over an hour.

Before long, I was joined by a crowd of school children. They surrounded me on all sides, and a few of the bolder ones proudly said "Good morning" in barely recognizable English. When I answered in Nande, they shouted with surprise, then laughed and peppered me with questions. They ran along beside me, chattering excitedly, and there was no getting rid of them. When I stopped, they stopped, and when I ran, they ran. Another hour went by like this, and by the time we finally reached their school, there were dozens and dozens of them, dancing along like some sort of victory celebration.

But it was 8:15 a.m. before I had anything to celebrate. Only then did I get a ride. A little pickup came speeding around a bend in the road and stopped in a swirl of dust. His truck was piled high with vegetables, kerosene, and passengers, but I was happy to get a lift. I climbed to the top of the heap and held on.

"Where you going?" he asked.

"Lukanga."

"Sorry," he said. "I can only take you to Lubero. You'll have to walk from there. We're going on to Butembo."

There are two roads to Butembo, branching off in separate directions at Lubero. The shorter one goes through Musienene, and the longer one goes through Lukanga. As a general rule, the trucks all take the shorter road, and for eleven months out of the year, we rarely see any traffic coming our way. Recently, though, because of the heavy rains, the road through Musienene had deteriorated badly, and most of the trucks were detouring through Lukanga. I had been over to Musienene myself to look at the bad spot in the road. It was impressive. There was a hole over eight feet deep and a hundred feet long. When it rained, the hole looked more like a lake.

"You'd better come around by Lukanga," I told the driver. "You'll never make it through Musienene."

He looked at me and laughed. You could hardly expect an unbiased report from someone who was looking for a ride to Lukanga.

"Only if it rains," he answered. "Otherwise I'll make it fine."

I looked at the sky. There were plenty of clouds, and I could tell there was a good chance of rain. Then I looked at my watch. At the rate these little pickups traveled, I might make it yet. But only if we went by Lukanga. From Lubero, it would be a three-hour walk.

"Lord," I prayed, "You've brought me this far, and I know you'll bring me the rest of the way. Please send the rain."

Nine o'clock came and went. No rain. Ten o'clock came and went, and ten-thirty. Still no rain. And then we were at Lubero. The little pickup stopped at the fork in the road and waited as I climbed down. The rain hadn't come.

"Sorry," said the driver. "We're going by Musienene."

I suppose one of the most frustrating aspects of the whole situation was that I knew he could never get through at Musienene. Sooner or later, he would have to turn around and come back this way, but that would be too late to be of any use to me. He would lose two hours and maybe more. He needed that rain just as badly as I did.

There was a moment's delay as the driver bargained for a few onions on sale by the side of the road. It was my last chance, and I made the most of it. I prayed.

"Sure could use a little rain, Lord."

The words were no sooner out of my mouth than the rain began to fall. It came in sheets. The driver grabbed his onions and ran to the truck. "All right," he said, looking at me in wonder, "you can get back on. We're going by Lukanga."

I needed no further invitation, and as I jumped back on, a prayer of thanks made its way back through the downpour and up to heaven.

The rain continued to come, drenching the earth and a few shivering passengers huddled miserably on the back of a pickup. Soon another prayer was working its way heavenward.

"Lord," I prayed, "could I ask just one more favor? You sent it when I needed it, but I don't need it anymore. Could You stop it? Please?"

For the second time in less than five minutes, my prayer was answered almost instantly. The rain stopped, and it didn't come again all the rest of the way to Lukanga. I arrived at eleven-fifteen, just in time, and I preached my farewell sermons.

There are those, I know, who wouldn't consider a ride and a five-minute downpour to be miracles. But I do. The rain came, not a minute too soon and not a minute too late, and lasted—only five minutes. A small thing, yes, but not a small miracle. After all, "There are no small miracles." Small lives and small people, maybe, but "that God should be interested in the little things of our little lives is a very big thing indeed."

Chapter 18

Till We Meet Again

It was half past midnight in the middle of nowhere, on the road that runs south from Lukanga. The clouds were spitting rain in my face, and the motorcycle was throwing up mud at my back.

"Half past midnight," I thought. "Monday already."

In six hours, we were scheduled to leave this all behind us and head back to North America. Yet here I was again, as I'd been two days before, racing against time over the very same road. And it was all my own fault. This time, there was nobody else to blame but myself.

I came to the conclusion that night, as I bumped and slipped over the muddy road, that there are two kinds of people in this world. There are those who go through life making the difficult seem easy, with never a wasted moment, never a backward glance; and then there are the rest of us, with a dubious gift for making the easy difficult and the difficult virtually impossible.

Call it a flair for living, if you're feeling charitable. Call it poor planning, if you're not. It doesn't really matter. The result is usually the same—every day's another adventure; nothing is ever routine. That's the way it was when I first came to Lukanga, and in spite of my best efforts, that's the way it has been ever since. And I realized now, with just hours until our departure, that's the way it would probably be to the very end.

I knew as well as anybody that this ride should never have been necessary, and it certainly wasn't something that I wanted to do. After my exhausting trip back from Goma, I had been looking forward to a day of rest and a chance to say Goodbye to my friends at my leisure. But it hadn't worked out that way.

When I left the truck on Friday night, I decided to be prudent and leave my passport and important papers locked up in the safety of the glove compartment. I had no idea where I'd be spending the night or if I'd be caught in the rain or if any of a dozen things might happen, and I wanted those papers to be kept in a perfectly safe place. It had all seemed so logical at the time.

"Sihingirwa," I had said melodramatically to one of the truck's occupants, "guard these papers with your life."

"*Ayyyyy,*" had been his casual response as he tossed the packet nonchalantly into the cab of the truck, "will do."

"Matthias," I said, turning to the truck driver, "when will you get back to Lukanga?"

"We should be in early Sunday morning," he answered.

"You know I'm leaving Monday?"

"No problem. We'll be there."

To ease my mind before I left, Sihingirwa put the papers securely in the glove compartment, and Mali, the truck driver's helper, locked the doors and stretched out on the seat. Usually, he slept in the back when the truck was on the road, so this would be an evening of luxury.

When I got back to Lukanga, I tried to put the truck out of my mind. But early Sunday morning, when I first woke up, I rushed up to the school to see if it had arrived. It hadn't.

Sunday slipped by in a whirl of work and visits. I kept an eye on the road, just in case, but the day went by with no sign of the truck.

Just before sundown at six, I held a final worship with the girls at the dorm. Then I went with Diane and the rest of the family, who had returned from North America, to a farewell supper in the school cafeteria. Still no sign of the truck. Now I was getting concerned. I knew Matthias and Mali and Sihingirwa too well. They were a lot like me. Nothing would keep them away from a free meal with all the rice and beans you could eat—not if they could help it. No, something was obviously wrong.

The evening passed by quickly. The food was good and the speeches were kind. After the supper was over, we stood around outside, shaking hands and hugging and fighting off the tears. It was ten o'clock before we made our way back home in the darkness. And at ten-fifteen, I was at the Bauers' house, knocking on the door.

"Eldon," I began.

"You want the bike," he said knowingly.

I nodded.

"You know I'd be happy to go for you," he offered.

"I know, but I couldn't ask you. And besides, I'd never get to sleep anyway."

He gave me the key. "I've already filled the tank," he said. "I figured you'd be coming."

I set off at once, hoping to see the truck at any time, but half afraid it was still sitting by the road where last I had seen it. I figured I could get there by three o'clock if that were the case, and if all went well. That would make the timing very close since Bob Roberts, our mission pilot, would want to be leaving by eight in the morning. Still, I'd been living with close timing every day for a week, and there was nothing to do but to try it and hope for the best.

Around every bend in the road, over every crest of a hill, I watched for those familiar headlights. And at one o'clock I saw them. The crew on the truck knew it was me even before I knew it was them. They'd been expecting me. They had spent the day scouring the countryside, looking at wrecked trucks and trying to find somebody somewhere to sell them the part that they needed, but it had been late in the afternoon before they'd finally been successful. They had made the repairs on the spot and then headed for home. They'd had no more sleep than I had had, but a promise was a promise—they were driving through the night to keep it.

Sihingirwa was the first one to greet me. He climbed down from the cab just as I was pulling off my mud-spattered helmet, and he called out as nonchalantly as if we'd met on a stroll across the lawn.

"What news?" he asked, as we reached to shake hands.

"No news, Sihingirwa."

"Are you awake?" he continued, as the Nande always ask.

"Yes," I replied, "I'm awake, but I'd much rather be in bed."

He laughed, then they brought me up to date about everything that had happened since I left them, and I told them everything that had happened to me. We chatted for a good fifteen minutes; then they gave me the papers, and I turned and headed for home. And had anyone been listening in the shadows, they would have thought from our casual manner that we met just like this all the time.

I got back to Lukanga just minutes before four. By six, there were visitors outside, friends who had walked down from some of the nearby churches. Soon there was a small crowd. Gad and Masinda, Katsyoto, and Kavira—and many, many more.

I would like to have said something eloquent before we drove off for the airstrip at Lubero, something which bespoke the bond which I felt with them all. Something which showed how happy we were that they'd opened their hearts to us and made us one of the family. But the words wouldn't come, so we shook hands all around and drove off in silence, waving and waving and waving.

We arrived at Lubero on time—more tears and more goodbyes. Then we climbed into the little mission plane. Bob Roberts said a prayer, as he always does before flying, then he taxied the plane down the grassy runway and took off.

We banked sharply to the right, with the hills of Lubero all around us; then we circled the valley several times to get enough altitude to go on. When we had gained sufficient height, Bob took off his headphones, turned in his seat, and shouted above the roar of the engine.

"Would you like to fly over Lukanga," he asked, "for a final goodbye?"

I nodded. "We'd like that very much."

And so we flew up to Lukanga, high above the classroom building. Around and around we went in a tight little circle.

Far below, the courtyard of the school was suddenly filled with students and teachers, spilling out from the classrooms and offices. All we could see were their faces turned upwards and hands waving high in the air.

We pressed our faces to the window and waved and waved and waved.

"Goodbye, Lukanga," I murmured. "Goodbye, dear friends." Then my eyes misted over, and the images below me grew blurred. Bob turned the plane toward Goma, and the school faded quickly from sight.

It was over. The best years of our lives had ended. I looked at Diane as she dabbed at her eyes, and we both reached out and held hands. Not a word passed between us, but this was a day on which words were not needed. I knew without asking that her thoughts were no different than mine. Lukanga was home, and we knew even then we'd be back. So it wasn't *adieu* we were saying, but *au revoir*—till we meet again, Lukanga; till we meet again, Zaire. God be with you till we meet again.